Sir Ganttalot®

Project Risk Management – a Rapid Rollout Methodology

Start Managing Project Risks Today!

Project Risk Management – a Rapid Rollout Methodology

Copyright © 2012 Westall Murray International, Inc.

All rights reserved. No part of this book shall be reproduced, stored in a retrieval system, or transmitted by any means, electronic, mechanical, photocopying, recording or otherwise without written permission from the publisher and author. No patent liability is assumed with respect to the use of the information contained therein. Although every precaution has been taken in the preparation of this book, the publisher and author assume no responsibility for errors or omissions. Nor is any liability assumed for damages resulting from the use of the information contained herein.

ISBN-13: 978-1-105-42023-8

Trademarks

All terms that are known to be trademarks or service marks have been appropriately identified as such on each usage. Westall Murray International, Inc. cannot attest to the accuracy of this information. Use of a term in this book should not be regarded as affecting the validity of any trademark or service mark.

The mark "Sir Ganttalot®" is a registered trademark of Westall Murray International, Inc.

Warning and Disclaimer

Every effort has been made to make this book as complete and accurate as possible, but no warranty or fitness is implied. This information is provided on an "as is" basis. The author and the publisher shall have neither liability nor responsibility to any person or entity with respect to loss or damages arising from the information or from the use of the information contained in this book.

Copyright and Usage Questions

Questions relating to copyright matters or regarding usage of this book should be directed to the copyright owner via email: info@westallmurray.com

Table of Contents

About Sir Ganttalot®   7

Introduction   8

Chapter 1: The Need for Project Risk Management   10

    What is Project Risk? 10

    What is Project Risk Management? 11

    Why Should YOU Deploy a Project Risk Management Methodology? 11

Chapter 2: An Overview of Sir Ganttalot's Rapid Rollout Methodology for Project Risk Management   14

    Step 1. Risk Identification 14

    Step 2. Risk Severity Assessment 15

    Step 3. Risk Response Formulation 16

    Step 4. Risk Control 17

    Step 5. Risk Review 17

    Relationships between the Steps in the Methodology 18

    Documenting your Overall Risk Approach 19

Chapter 3: Risk Identification   21

    The "Risk Log" 21

    Entering a Starter Set of Risks 22

    Working with Project Stakeholders to Capture Risks 23

    What Data is Captured during Risk Identification? 26

    Risk Identification – Roundup 28

Chapter 4: Risk Severity Assessment — 29

    The Purpose of Risk Severity Assessment 29

    A Combined Step! 30

    A Unique Concept: "Pre-Occurrence Manifestation" 31

    The Concept of Risk Probability 32

    Assessing Risk Probability in Practice 33

    The Concept of Risk Impact 34

    Assessing Risk Impact in Practice 35

    Using Probability and Impact to Determine Severity Level 36

    Assessing the Potential for Risk Pre-Occurrence Manifestation 37

    What Data is Added to the Risk Log during Risk Severity Assessment? 38

    Risk Severity Assessment – Roundup 38

    Chapter Postscript: Quantitative Risk Modeling 39

Chapter 5: Risk Response Formulation — 40

    The AIM of Risk Responses 40

    Primary Responses, Contingency Responses and Fallback Responses 40

    Types of Primary Risk Response 41

    Possible Primary Responses for NEGATIVE (Threat) Risks 41

    Possible Primary Responses for POSITIVE (Opportunity) Risks 42

    Examples of Primary Risk Responses in Practice – Threat Risk 43

    Examples of Primary Risk Responses in Practice – Opportunity Risk 45

Contingency Risk Responses 46

Conducting Expected Monetary Value (EMV) Analysis 47

Fallback Risk Responses 49

Responding to Risk Pre-Occurrence Manifestation. 49

Selecting Primary Responses, Contingency Responses and
Fallback Responses for YOUR Risks 49

(Sir Ganttalot Suggestion): 50

Caution: Beware of Secondary Risks! 50

Risk Response Formulation – Roundup 51

Chapter 6: Risk Control   53

Areas of Focus in Risk Control 54

Risk Control – Roundup 55

Chapter 7: Risk Review   56

Interaction with Risk Identification 56

Interaction with Risk Severity Assessment. 57

Interaction with Risk Response Formulation and with
Risk Control. 57

Additional Risk Review Activities 58

Risk Reporting 58

(Sir Ganttalot Suggestion): 60

Risk Review – Roundup 60

Chapter 8: Thoughts and Considerations for Project Risk Management   61

Epilogue   62

Appendix 1:

A Possible Schedule for Rolling Out Risk Management 63

Appendix 2:

Example of a Risk Log 66

Appendix 3:

Examples of Charts, Diagrams, and Reports used in Project Risk Management 68

Glossary / Index of Main Entries 72

About "Sir Ganttalot®"

Sir Ganttalot® is the alter-ego of Kelvin Murray, CEO of Westall Murray International, Inc., a Project Management consulting, services, training and staff augmentation company based in the Washington DC area of the USA. You can find Sir Ganttalot® on *YouTube®* delivering short training videos on Project Management topics, and you may well run into him at events, consulting engagements and training sessions across the US and worldwide.

Sir Ganttalot® has over 35 years' experience in Management, Leadership and Project Management positions, and has managed delivery of Project Management processes across six continents.

So why the moniker, "Sir Ganttalot®"? Well, Kelvin explained it one day when one of his team members came into his office and found him apparently having a quiet nap! Kelvin looked startled and related the following tale. It's hard to prove or disprove this story, so it's best just to take Kelvin's word for it. Kelvin explained,

"I was sitting here working on a project schedule when all of a sudden a blue ball of lighting came through the wall and nudged into me. Then, FLASH, some sort of time anomaly threw me back into the ancient kingdom of Wessex in the year 597! To survive, I found a job managing a castle construction project for King Calderwulf III. Naturally, the project was completed on time, within budget, and with all ramparts intact and fully functional. The King was delighted and dubbed me "Sir Ganttalot" on the spot! Then WHAM, the next thing I knew was here in the office, with you talking to me!"

What a strange story? Is it true? Well, we need more than Project Management skills to know for sure, so let's just humor the author for now....

To find out more about Westall Murray International's services and offerings, please visit www.WestallMurray.com, or go to YouTube® and search for Sir Ganttalot®.

Introduction

Many people looking to implement Project Management processes and procedures will obtain from the Project Management Institute® a copy of the book *"A Guide to the Project Management Body of Knowledge"*, often referred to as the *PMBOK® Guide* or simply as the *PMBOK®*. This is certainly a good starting point, in that the PMBOK® clearly explains the *knowledge* needed to implement the most common processes and procedures encountered on the majority of well managed projects.

The *PMBOK®* is not intended, though, to be a methodology. It simply explains what knowledge you need, and the inputs, tools and techniques, and outputs commonly found, in the operation of those common Project Management processes and procedures.

In order to get up and running with a particular Project Management discipline, such as Project Risk Management, you don't *just* need knowledge. What you need is a practical framework or methodology, with clearly defined steps and activities that can be readily understood by all the people involved in and associated with that discipline. More importantly you need a methodology that can be quickly implemented and which can be tailored easily to meet the specific needs of your project and its stakeholders.

In this book, I describe a Rapid Rollout Methodology for Project Risk Management. A methodology you can implement in a very short timeframe, and which can be readily understood and embraced by your stakeholders.

Perhaps you are working on a project, or have just joined a new project, and NO Risk Management is being done right now. Maybe your organization has just won a large piece of project-related work from a major client and your contract calls for you to deploy Risk Management as part of your services. For these and many other reasons, speed of implementation of a Project Risk Management capability may be a critical need. It is for such needs that Sir Ganttalot's, Rapid Rollout Methodology for Project Risk Management was created.

But wait, there's more! In addition to being a methodology that is easy and quick to deploy, **THIS methodology has some unique features missing from other Risk Management approaches**. Perhaps of most significance is the consideration of an additional Risk Response approach which I have called "Risk Precipitation". You will see the intent and value of this approach as part of your toolkit of other possible responses when you read about it in more detail in Chapter 5 of this book. In similar vein, a completely unique concept that I have titled "Pre-Occurrence Manifestation" is also introduced exclusively within this methodology.

Well, thanks for your interest in this fascinating topic, and in particular for choosing my book to help you. I wish you all success in your Risk Management endeavors.

Chapter 1

The Need for Project Risk Management

What is Project Risk?

Risks are uncertain occurrences or situations which, if they happen, will impact your project. The two core components of this definition are "uncertain" and "will impact".

Let's consider a simple example. You have embarked on a project to re-pave the driveway leading to your house. You have struck a deal with a friend who is a paving contractor. He will pave your driveway for the raw material cost of the asphalt, plus a fixed fee for his time and services. It's a good deal all round. Your friend needs some extra work to pay some family bills, and you want to get your driveway paved for less than the regular commercial rate. Based on your friend's estimate of the cost of the asphalt needed, even with his fee added on top, the price is very good indeed.

But there is some uncertainty, or Risk. The raw material cost of asphalt might INCREASE, making the total project cost too high to finish the complete driveway. On the other hand there is also a possibility that the cost of asphalt might go DOWN, meaning that the entire driveway project ends up costing less than expected, freeing up some spare funds for you to use on another project altogether.

From this example you can see that Risks can represent Threats, i.e. they can be NEGATIVE Risks, but they can sometimes represent Opportunities, i.e. they can be POSITIVE Risks.

These examples fit the definition of Project Risk at the start of this section, "Uncertain occurrences or situations which, if they happen, will impact your project". The raw material cost of asphalt might change, or it might not. But IF it changes, there will be an impact, good or bad, on your project.

And that brings us to the second component of the definition; "will impact". It is only uncertainty that will impact your project that you need to worry about. On the day your friend paves the driveway, you absolutely don't know whether or not there is a dust storm blowing on the northern slopes of the

Olympus Mons mountain on the planet Mars. You have absolute *uncertainty* about it. But in terms of your driveway, whether or not there is a sandstorm on Mars has no impact on your project at all. So you can safely omit any consideration of Martian sandstorms from your Risk Management activities!

Maybe the simplest way to think of Project Risk is along these lines,

"IF such-and-such happens, there WILL be consequences."

Accordingly, I will be using the term "**Consequential Uncertainty**" to characterize Project Risk and areas of Risk within a project.

What is Project Risk Management?

In Project Risk Management, your aim is to catalogue and evaluate areas of uncertainty in your project, and then to take steps to reduce Threats to the project and/or maximize the Opportunities on your project that arise from this uncertainty.

This means that you don't just identify and analyze possible Risks, you also need to do something about them. And you need to check continually to see whether your responses have achieved the desired effect. And of course, you must stay alert for new Risks, and review existing Risks, until your project is delivered.

Why Should You Deploy a Risk Management Methodology?

Well, if you do so everyone will immediately understand what you are doing, they will see the reasons for it and the potential benefits, and they will thank you for being the one to take the initiative. Don't believe me? Let me illustrate what I mean by coming at the point obliquely.

Let's imagine that you take a new job as a team member on a project in a new company. As always, your first two or three days are spent plodding your way through documentation to familiarize yourself with the project, with the client, with your new company, etc. Around Wednesday of your first week you are having a hard time staying alert, to say the least. All of a sudden a colleague stops by your cubicle and says, "Hey come on, we're all going to the weekly status meeting!"

PROJECT RISK MANAGEMENT – A RAPID ROLLOUT METHODOLOGY

Delighted with the interruption, you tag along to the conference room. Inside, the PM is at the head of the table and the dozen or so members of the project team are sitting at the table with a handout of papers in front of each person. You take a seat and pick up your handout. Without further ado, the PM looks around the table, "Welcome to the meeting everyone. I'd like to start right away with our EV metrics. Please turn to page 7 of your handouts. Right, Jane", (the PM delivers Jane a steely gaze, and launches into what sounds to you like Greek poetry), "I see the Tank Refinishing Control Account is still showing a CV of minus 200K and that the SV is getting worse, currently minus 327K. The projected EAC for this CA is 927K meaning a VAC of minus 234K. What's going on?"

At this point you are starting to wish you were still on your old project. Your mind is racing. What on earth are EV metrics? Please don't ask me anything, boss! Note to self....find out what EV is immediately after the meeting...Wikipedia here I come! Don't make eye contact! Hold on....the PM is speaking again...

"OK, let's move on to our Top 5 Risks.....Page 8 of your handouts. Susan, Risk Number 1 was assigned to you; the title is 'Withdrawal of Funding by the Sponsor leads to Project Cancellation'. We had this rated as Medium Probability, High Impact. At the last meeting you were assigned the task of speaking with the Sponsor, briefing her on project benefits and current status, and giving me feedback on the outcome. Did you have that meeting, Susan?"

"No, but we did have a brief talk in the cafeteria, and the Sponsor has agreed to meet with me for 40 minutes this afternoon."

The PM mulls this over for a moment, "OK, thanks for that. It is vital that this afternoon's meeting happens. Don't let me hear next week that it has been postponed again. In the meantime, do you think those ratings for Probability and Impact are still as shown?"

"Well", replies Susan, "Of course the Impact would still be high, total in fact, but based on the Sponsor's reaction in the cafeteria I would say that the Probability of funding withdrawal is pretty low, certainly not High as listed here in the Risk Register".

"OK", says the PM, "I'll drop it to Medium for now. Come and see me this afternoon after you meet with the Sponsor, please."

Now that's **better**! All of that was understandable. And indeed that's the whole point of this illustration. Risk Management makes sense, even the first time people are exposed to it. The benefits and purpose are self-explanatory. Of course, Risk Management can become very sophisticated indeed, and organizations can exhibit very different levels of maturity in their Risk Management approach. Nevertheless, implementing a Rapid Rollout of a basic Risk Management capability of the type discussed in this book can be done with minimum overhead, and the rewards will prove themselves in very short order.

So let's get to it, then! This book is all about deploying a workable, straightforward Risk Management Methodology quickly, allowing you to get started on Risk Management TODAY. Let me stop selling the idea of Risk Management, and tell you what you need to actually DO!

Chapter 2

An Overview of Sir Ganttalot's Rapid Rollout Methodology for Project Risk Management

Because Risk Management is a well-established project discipline, many other methodologies for Risk Management exist, and you will see similarities and common concepts reflected within them. In defining THIS particular methodology, my aim has been to present you with a quick start approach that can bring immediate results.

The methodology consists of a series of simple steps that will be repeated and revisited throughout the life of the project as necessary. These steps are:

1. Risk Identification
2. Risk Severity Assessment
3. Risk Response Formulation
4. Risk Control
5. Risk Review

The remaining chapters of this book address each of the steps of the methodology in detail. In this overview we will discuss these steps in brief, and make reference to a suggested timeline/schedule for implementation of the steps in a real project environment.

Step 1. Risk Identification

Once you have decided to move ahead with Risk Management you need to start determining the actual Risks and areas of Risk that may impact on your project. Central to the collection and recording of Risks will be the Risk Log. This document (probably a spreadsheet or database) will be the repository not just for the description of each Risk, but also for documenting your analysis of Risk severity, your selected control measures, and indeed all tracking and progress information relating to Risks and their management.

Risk Identification will require extensive tapping-in to the experience and expertise of a wide range of project stakeholders. Your own input regarding

Risks on the project is equally important, and in this Rapid Rollout Methodology you start by capturing your own set of Risks, which is valuable in its own right but which will also serve as a catalyst for ideas from those other stakeholders.

In Chapter 3 of this book the Risk Identification step in the Rapid Rollout Methodology is presented with tips, tricks and guidance to make your collection of Risks and your interaction with project stakeholders more effective.

Do remember above all that although Risk Identification is the first step in this Methodology, this does NOT mean that you perform Risk Identification just once. Risk Identification is a continuing, ongoing process. As your project unfolds, the project itself changes, and the uncertainty factors and potential uncertainty factors (good and bad) also change. So new Risks (both Threats and opportunities) will also arise. As a result of this you must revisit Risk Identification on a frequent and regular basis throughout your project.

Step 2. Risk Severity Assessment

In this step you look at each identified Risk to determine the magnitude of the Threat or Opportunity presented by the Risk. What you do is evaluate both the Probability of the Risk occurring and the extent of the Impact on the project (good or bad) if the Risk actually occurs.

As you will see in the detailed Chapter on this step (Chapter 4), in the Rapid Rollout Methodology you carry out both Qualitative Analysis and some limited Quantitative Analysis as a combined action. The purpose of this is to simplify and accelerate the rollout of Risk Management in a real project.

You also need to assess the extent of any "Pre-Occurrence Manifestation" of the Risk. This will allow you to deal with any effect on morale, behavior or performance of team members that the mere existence of the Risk might already be having within your project.

Once again your Risk Log is the document in which you will record the results of your Severity Assessments. The Risk Log can then at this point be sorted and/or grouped based on Risk Severity levels, allowing the next step in the Methodology, Risk Response Formulation, to be prioritized in cases where your available resources for Risk Management might be constrained or limited.

Step 3. Risk Response Formulation

Sadly, some organizations seem to think that Risk Management is complete once Risks have been identified and assessed. Then, when a disaster happens they take some small satisfaction from the fact that, "At least we captured that Risk!" Well of course capturing Risks is important, but even more importantly you need to *do something about the Risks*.

Exactly how you respond to a particular Risk depends on many factors, including the nature of the Risk itself, the resources and expertise you actually have available to address Risk overall, and your corporate acceptance of and/or sensitivity to Risk.

You may have heard or used the term "mitigate" as a word meaning "do something about Risks". Indeed, mitigation is the most common approach, but it is only one possible approach, and it only applies to Threat Risks, not to opportunities. In the Chapter on Risk Response Formulation (Chapter 5) we will discuss in detail other possible response strategies, such as transfer, precipitate, avoid, enhance, share and exploit. We will also consider the project factors and constraints that can steer you towards selecting an overall Risk Response policy as well as determining which specific Risk Responses are best for particular Risks in your Risk Log.

In addition to direct responses to a Risk, you might also choose to, or need to, identify Contingency Responses and/or Fallback Responses. So what are these?

A Contingency Response is something you plan ahead that you will do if the Risk actually happens. A Fallback Response is again something planned ahead of time, but you can think of it as a "Plan B". Fallback Responses are Responses you will implement if a Risk has a higher than expected impact, or if you determine that your primary Risk Responses are not having as great an effect on the Risk as you had intended.

Don't forget that formulating Primary, Contingency and Fallback Responses is all well and good, but you must also assign specific actions to individuals so that the responses can actually happen.

CHAPTER 2: OVERVIEW OF THE METHODOLOGY

Step 4. Risk Control

Let's take stock. At this point, for just one specific Risk, if you have performed the steps in the Methodology so far you will have the Risk identified and described in your Risk Log. You will also have determined the overall severity of the Risk in terms of Probability of occurrence, and Impact on your project in the event that it happens. And you will also have formulated one or more Risk Responses. So, is that the end of the story? The answer of course, is a very firm, "NO!"

Just because your Risk Log contains Risk Responses doesn't mean that the assigned individuals will actually implement them. They may get diverted onto other tasks, or they might simply overlook the assigned actions altogether. It may be that the assigned people don't have the ability, resources, skills or expertise to implement the actions. Even in cases where the actions are being carried out, you need to ensure that the actions are indeed having the desired effect on the Risks concerned.

Risk Control, then, means going beyond planning your approach to Risks, and actually starting implementing the assignments within the Risk Response Plans. And whenever you start doing something on a project, whether it's controlling Risks or performing any other project or Project Management task, you must ensure that the tasks are executed and monitored, and where necessary modified, to ensure that those tasks are having the required effect.

Step 5. Risk Review

This last step in the methodology is of course not really "last" at all. As mentioned earlier, all of the steps in the Methodology are repeated and performed as necessary throughout a project. What do we mean, then, by Risk Review?

Both for individual Risks and for the overall realm of Risks on your project, you absolutely must ensure that your Risk Log is complete, current and accurate.

As the project progresses, new Risks are likely to arise. Some Risks stop being Risks altogether. Perhaps their time has come and gone. If they were to happen now, there might be no impact at all. For other Risks, maybe your Risk Responses have had sufficient effect such that the Risk can be closed.

PROJECT RISK MANAGEMENT – A RAPID ROLLOUT METHODOLOGY

Other areas to review in the Risk Log include addressing questions such as whether the description is still valid. What about your Severity Assessment? Are the Risk Responses still relevant and appropriate? Do some Risks need to be allocated to a different Category from the one currently listed?

From the above it is probably apparent to you that this step in the Methodology, Risk Review, and the previous step, Risk Control, are complementary and concurrent processes. Controlling Risks by nature will modify the Risks themselves and the data associated with the Risks. Likewise, as you Review Risks, you uncover information that might lead to a need to modify the current Control measures that you are applying to specific Risks.

Relationships between the Steps in the Methodology

So we have 5 steps in the methodology, and as I have stated several times these steps are repeated as and when necessary throughout the life of the project. Nevertheless there is a logical relationship between the steps that can help you visualize when and how you should carry out specific actions relating to individual Risks.

Understanding this set of relationships between the steps is helpful to us in planning and scheduling specific Risk Workshops and Risk Review Sessions as part of your overall Project Management activities. Interactions between the Methodology Steps can be visualized as shown in Figure 1, below:

Figure 1: Relationship between the Methodology Steps

CHAPTER 2: OVERVIEW OF THE METHODOLOGY

Based on an understanding of the interaction between the Methodology Steps as shown in Figure 1, it is possible to plan and schedule your specific Risk Management tasks and activities for your project.

Exactly *when* various Workshops and other actions need to happen will vary from project to project, based on factors such as the total value of the project and its duration, what the range of stakeholders is and who they all are, how much funding and time is available for Risk Management, where the various stakeholders and members of the project team are located, and on many other considerations. As a starting point for your own planning, we have included a suggested generic schedule for Risk Management tasks and activities in Appendix 1 of this book. Remember, this schedule is deliberately high level and generic; it is not proscriptive. You should elaborate on it and modify it as necessary to meet the needs of your project

Documenting *your* Overall Risk Approach

Those of you familiar with the PMI's *PMBOK® Guide* might want to equate the steps in this Rapid Rollout Methodology for Project Risk Management with the overall *PMBOK® Guide* explanation of Risk Management Processes. There is most definitely not a one-to-one match, primarily because *the PMBOK® Guide* is not itself a *methodology* of any kind. It is what it is: a Body of Knowledge. It recommends that you have and use a methodology, but it does not give you a specific methodology.

Indeed, the *PMBOK® Guide* includes as one of its "processes" an ongoing action called "Plan Risk Management". In part, by deciding to deploy a Methodology for Risk Management you have already performed some Risk Management Planning. You have decided that Risk Management is necessary and you have decided to deploy Sir Ganttalot's Rapid Rollout Methodology.

But simply deciding to implement Risk Management isn't quite all the planning that you need to do. You have to determine how much Risk Management is needed. You need to identify roles and responsibilities for Risk Management. You need to determine the timing of the various Tasks and Activities associated with your selected Rapid Rollout Methodology. You need to determine how much time, effort, resources and money you can afford to expend on Risk Management, and you need to budget accordingly.

PROJECT RISK MANAGEMENT – A RAPID ROLLOUT METHODOLOGY

You also need to make sure that your Risk Management Methodology interfaces well with all of your other Project Management activities.

Planning for all aspects of your project continues *throughout* your project, you don't simply plan everything ahead of time and plow on regardless. When the project changes, your plans probably need to change as well. So don't overlook the need to document thoroughly your Risk Management approach within your overall master Project Management Plan (PMP) documentation. And be sure to revisit and update your overall approach, and to update the PMP as needed, as your project unfolds.

Let's close out this Chapter now. We have seen a short overview of what the Rapid Rollout Methodology for Project Risk Management consists of, and we have discussed what the Methodology is seeking to achieve. We have seen how the steps in the Methodology relate to one another. We have described the need to document your specific approach to Risk Management within your Project Management Plan, and we have addressed the need to plan in detail the timing of Risk Management Tasks and Activities. But all of that was just an overview. The remaining chapters in this book address each of the steps in Sir Ganttalot's Rapid Rollout Methodology for Project Risk Management in more detail, including guidance on the techniques and approaches necessary to perform each step.

Chapter 3
Risk Identification

This step (which is repeated as needed throughout the project) captures and documents Risks for a particular project. As Risks are captured they are entered into the Risk Log. The Risk Log becomes the action repository for not merely listing the Risks, but also for tracking all management activities related to the Risks. Put another way, you will update the Risk Log at every stage of the Rapid Rollout Methodology.

The "Risk Log"

Risk Logs can take the form of a spreadsheet, a database or perhaps may be maintained within a collaboration software application such as Microsoft® SharePoint®. Typically there will be one "entry" (spreadsheet row, for example) for each identified Risk. Sir Ganttalot's recommended set of columns/fields for each Risk entry is shown below. **NOTE** that when you *first* identify a Risk you will *not* be able to enter information into *every* column. Several of the columns are there for use/completion in subsequent steps in the Methodology. During initial Risk Identification, only the items in italics in this list are likely to be entered:

- *Risk Serial Number*
- *Risk Title*
- *Risk Description*
- *Risk Category*
- *Threat/Opportunity (T/O)*
- Probability
- Impact
- Pre-Occurrence Manifestation
- Risk Severity Level

- *Trigger (optional)*
- Primary Risk Response Type
- Primary Risk Response Details
- Primary Risk Response Progress and Comments
- Response Owner
- Contingency Response
- Fallback Response
- *Date Raised*
- *Status*
- Date Closed

As you get rolling on Risk Management you may see a need to modify or supplement this set of columns.

(An example of a Risk Log page using the columns listed above, with data for an example Risk entered, is included in Appendix 2. Note that the example Risk Log shows a Risk that has been Identified and then taken through the other steps in the Rapid Rollout Methodology for Project Risk Management. For newly-identified Risks, some of the columns would be blank until later stages of the Methodology have been completed.)

Entering a Starter Set of Risks

So you have a Risk Log, but right now it is empty! How do you actually identify Risks to put into the log? Well, remember that a Risk is an area of uncertainty with potential impact (good or bad) on your project. To identify areas of *consequential uncertainty*, you need to have a good understanding of what your project is all about, and of the factors relating to and impinging on your project. So start by reflecting your OWN understanding of these areas, and ENTER SOME RISKS YOURSELF. Having done this you can start the process of engaging with other project stakeholders to get their input. Undoubtedly some of the stakeholders won't understand what you are looking for, but you have a secret weapon! You have a Risk Log with your starter set of Risks listed. As we mentioned earlier, when people see Risk Management in action they quickly grasp the concept. So show them the Risk Log!

But of course you may still be at a loss as to how to even enter that starter set of Risks. Here, then, are some immediate aspects of the project to review and scrutinize for possible areas of *consequential uncertainty*:

- **All *estimates***. By definition, estimates for cost, duration, work effort, scope, etc. have inherent uncertainty. If they were certain, they would be facts, not estimates.

- **Your project schedule**, in particular major dependencies within and external to your project. Events that you are depending on to happen just might not actually happen!

- **Key project documents**, especially any that list *assumptions*. Once again, assumptions are by nature ways of expressing uncertainty. You would not have documented them as assumptions if they were absolutes.

- **Contracts** awarded to sub-contractors or vendors.

- **Service Level Agreements** with other internal departments for the provision of services and/or staff.

Working with Project Stakeholders to Capture Risks

Armed with at least a few Risks that you have identified and logged yourself you can now begin interacting with other project stakeholders to get their take on the Risks associated with your project. In some cases you may meet one-on-one with specific people, and in other cases you may choose or need to interact with several stakeholders at once.

When you interact with stakeholders, you are seeking input from them. Capturing information on possible Risks is fundamentally no different from capturing requirements, capturing cost estimates, getting information about project tasks and activities, or indeed about anything on which you need input. This means that many of the specific tools, techniques and methods you use for general information gathering work just as well for gathering Risk-related data. Here are some approaches which have worked well for me, and which I recommend as possible methods for Risk Identification to include in your own Rapid Rollout of Risk Management:

- **One-on-One Interviews**. This is probably the approach to take with your more senior or influential stakeholders. Such people rightly expect you to come to them if you need some of their valuable time. Most probably that time will be limited, so make sure you prepare ahead of time to make the session as productive as possible. Make sure you tell them in advance the purpose of the visit. Consider sending them a starter set of Risks to stimulate their thoughts, but try not to stifle their own creativity by doing so. Even though you have prepared them ahead of time, remember they still may not have read your messages or thought much about the session before you show up, so expect that you may need to explain the purpose and aims of the visit all over again when you arrive. Possibly prepare a short "elevator speech" that describes the aim of the session in 45 seconds or less.

- **The Delphi Technique**. In this technique you seek input from a small group of individuals one at a time, possibly via email. You may, for example, ask each person to submit their top 5 Risks. You then consolidate and scrub the inputs to create a joint list of Risks which you send back to each person, asking for updated thoughts. You repeat the cycle as many times as practical/necessary until you have a consensus view on project Risk. Such a technique allows people to submit "anonymous" input in the sense that you don't indicate WHO suggested each Risk. This can help overcome some peoples' natural reluctance to publicly air their own perceived "problems", or their own perceptions of Risks arising from other areas or stakeholders.

- **Workshops and Working Groups**. There are times when it helps to interact with more than one stakeholder at a time. Sometimes group dynamics are what you need to generate a more comprehensive set of Risks, and to get more immediate cross-functional ideas about specific Risks or about Risks in general for your project. When groups of people get together you often find that you need to stimulate creativity, or at least get the ball rolling a little. Helpful methods for prompting and then making sense of the input can include:

- **Brainstorming**. This approach means more than just having a meeting. You would introduce the session by saying something like this,

    "OK everyone; I want fast, furious input, as much as possible. I don't care about ranks, positions, the fact that someone's a VP or a code developer. And I don't want to hear anyone say, "No", or "I disagree" or "That's a bad idea". Instead, feed on one another's input. Use input and ideas to create more ideas!"

    Sadly this can have too good an effect and you end up with way too much input. So it may be helpful to try to make sense of, or categorize, some of the Risks you have uncovered, using some of the remaining techniques in this list.

- **Mind Mapping and "Cause and Effect Diagrams"**. If someone suggests a Risk, you may decide that there could be underlying Risks or contributing factors at a more detailed level that could be important to tease out of the group. Some helpful methods in such a case could be to use Cause and Effect (Ishikawa) or Mind Map diagrams. An example of an Ishikawa diagram and a description of a Mind Map are included in Appendix 3.

- **Affinity Diagrams**. These diagrams are essentially a way to group related concepts together. One example might be to record key thoughts on sticky notes that you can arrange and re-arrange into groups and categories on a whiteboard or wall as discussion unfolds.

- **Sensitivity Analysis**. You will be performing detailed Risk Severity Assessment as a *later* stage in the Rapid Rollout Methodology. Nevertheless, while you have a group of stakeholders together for Risk Identification purposes, it may be useful to get their ideas on how "sensitive" aspects of the project might be to one or more of your identified Risks. You might want to make use of Tornado Diagrams as part of this early "analysis". An example of a Tornado Diagram can be found at Appendix 3.

PROJECT RISK MANAGEMENT – A RAPID ROLLOUT METHODOLOGY

What Data is Captured during Risk Identification?

Risk Identification is the process whereby you capture information about a Risk and about is relationship to your project. You don't assess Risk severity or formulate Risk Responses in this step of the Methodology. All of that takes place in subsequent steps. So what data **do** you capture in this step?

The following areas should be addressed and entered into your Risk Log before you move from Risk Identification into later stages of Risk Management:

- **Risk Serial Number**. Make sure you have a clear numbering system for your Risks. When conducting Risk Review meetings later in the Methodology you will need to be able to discuss specific Risks readily and easily. Being able to saying to the assembled stakeholders, "Please look at Risk Number 5-2 on Page 6 of your handouts" is a lot easier than having them look for specific Risk Titles, especially where several Risks might have very similar titles. Also, in some Risk Software Applications (including custom database or spreadsheet applications you may create yourself); Risk Serial Number will probably serve as your best "key field".

- **Risk Title**. The Title of a Risk is usually a summarized version of the Risk Description (see the next item). Be sure to state the Title in a way that makes it unique from other similar Risks.

- **Risk Description**. It is best to use an "if-then" formulation when entering the Risk Description. This helps to ensure that you only capture Risks that you care about, i.e. those that impact your project and truly represent areas of *consequential uncertainty*. To illustrate the point briefly here, let's consider an area of Risk such as, say, Janet Alexander resigning from the company. One of the Risks you might choose to document in this case could be, "*Janet Alexander resigns from the company resulting in 6 weeks of delay in completion of testing due to the need to secure a replacement Tester and bring that person up to speed*".

- **Risk Category**. When you first ask people about their ideas regarding Risks on a project, many of them will respond with rather high level areas of Risk, rather than one or more cleanly-formatted "if-then" statements. Someone might say, "Staff Turnover" for example. Don't be too quick to discard such comments. In many cases what people are expressing is a Category of Risk, within which many specific Risks could later come to light. So, not only capture and consolidate these "areas" or Categories of Risk, but build on them to compile a formal list of Risk Categories and make sure you assign each individual Risk to a Risk Category. This will allow you to filter, group or sort your Risks by Risk Category if needed for specific, subsequent, Risk Workshops or Focus Group sessions.

Your list of Risk Categories is likely to evolve over time. No single list of Risk Categories is likely to apply across all types of project. Nevertheless, here are some *examples* of Risk Categories to stimulate your own identification and selection of Risk Categories: *Personnel, Technology, Sub-contractors, Environment, Client; Organization; Political Considerations; Marketplace* and more. Many of these might have sub-categories. It is fairly common for organizations to depict Risk Categories and sub-Categories and even Parent Categories in the form of a tree, like an Organization Chart but showing the hierarchy of Risk Categories. Such a diagram is often referred to as a Risk Breakdown Structure (RBS). An example RBS is illustrated in Appendix 3.

- **Threat or Opportunity?** This is simply a "flag" to show whether a specific Risk represents a Threat or an Opportunity, so a value of T or O would be entered. You may be thinking that a particular area of Risk could possibly represent either a Threat OR an Opportunity, depending on "how things pan out". In such cases I recommend that you record separate Risks with appropriate "if-then" statements in the Risk Description, rather than try to cover too many scenarios with a single Risk.

- **Trigger** (Optional). Some organizations will choose to identify and record one or more "Trigger" events or indicators for a Risk. A Trigger is an event or circumstance that will indicate to you that the Risk is now happening or is about to happen. In other words, how will you know when the Risk is moving from being a Risk and becoming a real live project Issue? In fact why would you need to know anyway? Well, when the Risk actually starts to manifest itself, that will be your "trigger" to initiate any Contingency Responses that you identified for a Risk (you will address Contingency Responses in

Step 3 – Formulate Risk Responses, see Chapter 5). Basically, when the Trigger event happens, all *Uncertainty* associated with whether the Risk will happen has gone away. Now the Risk is here, so we need to address the *Consequences* of the occurrence.

- **Date Raised**. This is a self-explanatory field. In addition to its obvious necessity, you may possibly need to sort Risks by Date Raised during Step 5 of the Methodology, "Risk Review" so that you can review the longer-standing Risks first, or maybe review them last, depending on your approach.

- **Status**. It can be helpful to quickly identify Risks by various types of Status, such as *Open, Active, Closed, Materialized,* etc. Be creative and determine Status values that reflect the way you want to manage your Risks. As with all such sets of values, a Status field allows you to group, sort, or filter your Risks by these criteria for specific reviewing or reporting needs.

Risk Identification – Roundup

As you get ready to move on from your first round of Risk Identification, you will be armed with a set of Risks in your Risk Log. For these Risks you will have captured a fair amount of data about what the Risks are and how they relate to your project. But you need more information about the Risks than this. You need to move to a situation where you are planning to address the Risks, and the first step on that path is to Assess the Severity of each Risk. We will discuss this in our next Chapter, which covers Step 2 in the Rapid Rollout Methodology for Project Risk Management: Risk Severity Assessment.

Chapter 4

Risk Severity Assessment

The Purpose of Risk Severity Assessment

Have you *ever* worked on a project where you had unlimited resources and you could do every activity to whatever level of perfection you needed to, no questions asked? Almost certainly not! You have to work within your available budget, you often have a fixed team of people, and you only have the luxury of a certain amount of time to address each aspect of Project Management. This holds true for Risk Management as well. There is only so much Risk Management capacity available, but oh so many Risks to address! You need to be absolutely sure that your resources for Risk Management are expended to the greatest effect, and to do that you need to determine the relative severity of your Risks so that you can prioritize your responses.

Before proceeding, let's briefly remind ourselves of how Risk Severity Assessment relates to the other steps in the Rapid Rollout Methodology.

Figure 2: Relationship between Risk Severity Assessment and the Other Methodology Steps

A Combined Step!

In many Risk Management methodologies you will find that Risk Analysis is broken into two steps: *Qualitative Risk Analysis and Quantitative Risk Analysis.*

The first of these, Qualitative Analysis, is an overall assessment of the magnitude of a Risk, usually performed by assessing values for Probability of Risk occurrence, and of the Impact of the Risk, in general terms. For example, the Probability of a Risk happening might be rated on a three-point scale as High, Medium or Low. Or perhaps values of Likely, Possible and Unlikely might be used. Sometimes a rating on a scale of 1 through 5, or 1 through 10, with 1 being lowest might be used.

Also in Qualitative Analysis, a value for Risk Impact is determined, and once again a three-point scale such as High, Medium or Low, or for Risk Impact a scale of Severe, Moderate and Low. As with Probability, a numeric rating could be used, such as 1 through 5, or 1 through 10. The reason that numeric scales are sometimes used is so that a Risk Score (an overall Risk severity) can be calculated by simply multiplying the probability number by the impact number P x I. A variant is to multiply Probability by two times the Impact, i.e. P x (2 x I).

In a few organizations Quantitative Analysis is also performed on some Risks. In this more complex analysis, hard numbers for Impact on cost and/or schedule are determined. In other words a Risk is assessed for how MANY weeks delay would result, and/or how MANY extra dollars would be needed to deal with the fallout from a Risk.

Now there are a couple of issues with splitting analysis into two components this way, especially for people wanting to deploy a Rapid Rollout Methodology for Risk Management. Firstly, even just determining a qualitative assessment of impact does require some understanding of the impact on cost and/or schedule anyway. What exactly is a High impact on Cost? For some organizations it could be anything over $1,000.00, whereas for other organizations a $1,000.00 impact could be trivial. So in a sense, to do Qualitative Analysis, some degree of Quantitative Analysis is involved as well.

Another issue with splitting out Quantitative Analysis is that it to do Quantitative Analysis to any depth, you really need to consider using modeling applications or specialist software, possibly using Monte Carlo simulation that go beyond the scope of a Rapid Rollout Methodology.

So, in THIS methodology I have consolidated the key features of Qualitative and Quantitative Risk Analysis into a single step, "Risk Severity Assessment". Although it is a single Methodology Step, a number of related tasks, activities, techniques and artifacts will form part of this single "step".

A Unique Concept: *"Pre-Occurrence Manifestation"*

In this Rapid Rollout Methodology I have reflected an aspect of Risk Management that is completely omitted from other methodologies. Indeed I am convinced that this concept is unique to this methodology. The concept is simple, but vital if we aim to truly reflect the effect of uncertainty on a project. The term I will use is *"Pre-Occurrence Manifestation"*.

By *Pre-Occurrence Manifestation* I mean the effect that the mere awareness of the existence of a Risk can have now, right here in the present, even though the Risk Event is still uncertain. Sometimes, just knowing that a situation is a risky one can impact on our behavior, our morale and our attitudes within a project; even if in the end the Risk never transpires at all.

To illustrate this idea, let's consider one of those "ropes course" adventure parks, where sometimes groups from offices and projects go for "team building" activities. You may know what I mean. You have to negotiate obstacles and planks to traverse a route through the trees many feet off the ground. You come to a plank that is maybe 12 inches wide. It forms a bridge between two platforms in the trees, and there is a drop of 75 feet or so beneath it. You are wearing a harness, but nevertheless crossing the chasm is daunting. Anyway, you set off nervously, lose your balance, and fall off. You get lowered to the ground by the instructor in front of all your friends! But if that same plank had been lying on the ground, you could have crossed it 50 times without trouble. You could have hopped, skipped or danced across, forwards or backwards. You could have crossed wearing a blindfold.....because there was no perceived Risk! But up in the air, with friends watching and the threat of a fall from on high, you were almost doomed to failure!

Within your project, as part of your Risk Severity Assessment, you must address potential Pre-Occurrence Manifestations of a Risk in order to truly determine the interaction of the Risk with your project and your project team. Pre-Occurrence Manifestation in a project context is addressed further a little later in this Chapter.

The Concept of Risk Probability

Assessing Risk Probability means determining how likely it is that a particular Risk will occur. Probability represents the "uncertainty" element of Sir Ganttalot's term, *"Consequential Uncertainty"* used to refer to Project Risk.

Various rating scales are possible, but we have chosen a 3 point rating of High, Medium and Low for the Rapid Rollout Methodology. Inevitably some readers will ask at this point, "What do High, Medium and Low actually mean in practice?" Well at this point the answer has to be, "It depends!", but I can add some specifics that can help you determine levels for your project.

There is actually nothing wrong with leaving High, Medium and Low with qualitative definitions, and simply working on stakeholders' and your own "best estimate" within that qualitative scale. In everyday life, most people would understand if you were to say there is a High chance that you will resign from your job this week, just as much as they would understand if you said there was a Low chance. It is unlikely that you would say there is a "71%" chance or some other firm number. So a simple consensus agreement that a particular project Risk has a High, or Low, or Medium chance of happening may be enough for some Risk Management approaches.

In some cases though you may have a need to allocate a firm percentage for probability, particularly in cases where you intend to carry out not just Response Planning but also detailed Contingency Planning (See Chapter 5, Risk Response Formulation). The reason for this is that determining your required level of Contingency Reserve funds or time will make use of a technique called Expected Monetary Value (EMV) Analysis (again, see Chapter 5), and for EMV analysis you need detailed probability percentages.

So how can you cover both possibilities? Simply put, you classify High, Medium and Low probabilities as equating to bands of percentage probabilities as shown in the table on the following page (Figure 3):

CHAPTER 4: RISK SEVERITY ASSESSMENT

QUALITATIVE PROBABILITY VALUE	EQUIVALENT PROBABILITY % RANGE
HIGH	> 67%
MEDIUM	33% to 67%
LOW	< 33%

Figure 3: Example of a Risk Probability Table

This table may suffice simply as shown for projects or specific Risks where Contingency EMV Analysis will <u>not</u> be performed at any point. In the event that EMV analysis <u>is</u> anticipated, then either as part of this step, or during Step 3, Formulate Risk Responses, an additional level of detailed analysis of probability, down to a specific percentage vale, can be performed as needed. **NOTE.** Remember that Risks can represent Threats (Negative Risks) and Opportunities (Positive Risks) within your project!

Assessing Risk Probability in Practice

So much for the concept, but how do you <u>determine</u> the value for Probability for a particular Risk? It comes down to a combination of expert opinion and historical fact. You need to revisit your stakeholders, possibly via Risk Workshops or perhaps through one-on-one sessions to get individual and/or consensus estimates for Probability. Many of the techniques we discussed under Risk Identification (Chapter 3) for interacting with and gaining input from stakeholders can also be useful when attempting to get stakeholder assessments for Risk Probability.

Potentially you can also mine into hard data about Risks that applied to other projects. Remember, a Risk is an uncertain event for your own project, but if a similar event actually DID happen elsewhere on other projects, and maybe did NOT happen on yet other projects, you can analyze such occurrences as part of the assessment of the likelihood of that event happening in your own case.

At the very least, historical data might help us validate and/or challenge stakeholder "gut feel" assessments. If a stakeholder tells us that a particular Risk has a High Probability, but your own research shows that such an event has never happened in any of, say, 35 projects, then you will need to reconcile the apparent discrepancy.

Assume at this point, then, that you have taken several Risks in the Risk Log and assigned ratings of High, Medium or Low as your assessment of the Probability of those Risks occurring. As part of overall Severity Assessment you also need to assess the level of Impact on your project if those Risk events were actually to take place.

The Concept of Risk Impact

Assessing Risk Impact means determining the extent of the effect on your project if a particular Risk event were actually to occur. Impact represents the "consequences" element of Sir Ganttalot's term, *"Consequential Uncertainty"* to refer to Project Risk.

As with Risk Probability, here in the case of Risk Impact there are various scales that could be used to assign Impact values. Again, we have selected a three point scale of High, Medium and Low. It is at this point that the Rapid Rollout Methodology brings together elements of two separate levels of analysis, *Qualitative Risk Analysis* and *Quantitative Risk Analysis*. The reason for this is that in order to allocate an assessment of High, Medium or Low in terms of Impact (which is simply Qualitative Analysis), you need to know what High Medium and Low impacts actually mean in practice. You need to have some appreciation for the likely size of the impact in monetary, time, or functionality terms. This understanding is essentially a form of Quantitative Analysis.

In the Rapid Rollout Methodology, then, your assessment of Risk Impact is a combination of Qualitative Analysis with some limited Quantitative Analysis wrapped in with it. Note that it MAY be necessary to perform more detailed Quantitative Analysis on specific Risks IF you intend to carry out Expected Monetary Value Analysis (as discussed earlier in this section) as part of more detailed Contingency Planning within Step 3 of the Methodology, *Risk Response Formulation*.

Alright, let's look at how you actually conduct this combined analysis as part of your Severity Assessment. The first step is to put together an Impact Assessment Key similar to the example in Figure 4. The reason for saying "similar" is that all the values in this key will be dependent on the nature of your specific project. A HIGH cost impact on one project could be anything over $1,000.00, whereas on another project such a cost impact could be trivial.

IMPACT RATING	COST IMPACT	TIME (SCHEDULE) IMPACT	FUNCTIONALITY/ SCOPE/ PERFORMANCE IMPACT
HIGH	> $50,000.00	> 10 Weeks	> 50%
MEDIUM	$15,000.00 to $50,000.000	2 Weeks to 10 Weeks	15% to 50%
LOW	< $15,000.000	< 2 Weeks	< 15%

Figure 4: Example of an Impact Assessment Key

Assessing Risk Impact in Practice

Equipped with a table such as the one in the above example you can start interacting with stakeholders to get individual and/or consensus estimates for Impact. Although in this book we have discussed Probability and Impact as separate elements, almost certainly you will be collecting both Probability and Impact assessments from stakeholders at the same time, again, possibly via Risk Workshops or perhaps through one-on-one sessions.

As with Probability, you can also mine into hard data about the Impact that Risks actually had on other projects. If a particular event actually DID happen elsewhere on other projects, and you have identified a Risk that a similar event may happen on your own project, you can perhaps use the Impact on that other project as part of your own Impact assessment.

Likewise, historical data might help us validate and/or challenge stakeholder Impact assessments. When a stakeholder tells us that a particular Risk will have a high Impact, but your own research shows that Impact on other projects was minor, then you will need to investigate further and decide exactly how the Risk needs to be reflected regarding potential impact on your own project.

Using Probability and Impact to Determine Severity Level

With 3 levels of Probability and 3 levels of Impact, you immediately have 9 possible permutations that any Risk could have for its Risk/Impact assessment. You will of course enter the assessments for both values into the Risk Log entry for a particular Risk. But once the values are entered for, say 75 Risks, where will you now prioritize your attention? Which Risks are most important? Is a Risk with Medium Probability High Impact more severe than a Risk with High Probability Medium Impact? Or is it the other way around? Or are they equally severe?

Rather than have 9 permutations to baffle you, you may choose to make use of a Risk Severity Grid to determine what Severity Level you will assign to each Risk. Determining a Severity Level is important because it allows us to determine the degree of response needed during Step 3, Risk Response Formulation (See Chapter 5).

Sir Ganttalot suggests a 3-Level system for use within the Rapid Rollout Methodology:

Level 1 ("Red") Risks are the most severe Risks. For these you will develop Primary Responses, Contingency Responses and Fallback Responses in Step 3, Risk Response Formulation.

Level 2 ("Yellow") Risks are of Medium severity. These will require a Primary Response and a Contingency Response as a minimum.

Level 3 ("Blue") Risks are Low in severity. These are likely to be moved to the "Watch List" section of the Risk Log, as discussed later in this Chapter.

Those are the Severity Levels. Let's take a look at how you allocate each Risk to a Severity Level. First you need to create a Risk Severity Grid that will be used for your particular project. The example at Figure 5 on the following page is just that, an example. You are absolutely free to modify it to meet your own preferences for Severity Levels, or indeed in any other way necessary to create the best fit for your needs.

CHAPTER 4: RISK SEVERITY ASSESSMENT

PROBABILITY			
High	Level 2 / Yellow	Level 1 / Red	Level 1 / Red
Medium	Level 3 / Blue	Level 2 / Yellow	Level 1 Red
Low	Level 3 / Blue	Level 3 / Blue	Level 2 / Yellow
IMPACT	Low	Medium	High

Figure 5: Example of a Risk Severity Grid

To use the Risk Severity Grid, simply take any Risk in the Risk Log and read off the values you assigned for Probability and Impact. Let's say Risk number 17 in your Risk Log has a Probability of Medium and an Impact of High. This means that Risk 17 currently "belongs" in the cell in the Risk Severity Grid where Medium Probability and High Impact intersect, and so it has a Severity Assessment of Level 1 / Red.

Repeat this assessment for all Risks where you have assigned values for Probability and Impact, and allocate a Severity Level to all of them.

Note. In practice you can fairly easily put together a formula or macro within your Risk Log application (whether it be a spreadsheet, a database, or maybe in Microsoft® SharePoint®) that calculates the Risk Severity Level based on the values you enter for Impact and Probability.

Assessing the Potential for *Risk Pre-Occurrence Manifestation*

As discussed earlier, Pre-Occurrence Manifestation of a Risk refers to potential effects that the mere existence and awareness of a Risk might have, or may already be having, on the morale, behavior or performance of your project team. Because such potential effects are less measurable in terms of scale or of likelihood than direct effects of the Risk itself if it were to actually happen, assessing Pre-Occurrence Manifestation relies heavily on your overall Project Management, general management and people skills.

You must remain alert for signs and signals arising from team behavior or from project performance data that indicate that these are being influenced by less-than-tangible causes (such as the awareness of a Project Risk). Be aware also that it is not just Negative, or Threat Risks that can have this type of backward-impact. The existence of Positive, Opportunity Risks can create a climate of overconfidence or rashness that could in turn lead to sloppy attention to detail and poor quality of project deliverables. Team members could be thinking, "Well, it doesn't matter if I do a slap-dash job on this task, there are so many opportunities in this project that the results of any slip-up by me will be made up elsewhere". The problem is, of course, that if *all* the team members think and behave this same way the project is heading for trouble very quickly.

Recording of your assessment of Pre-Occurrence Manifestation will take the form of narrative descriptions of potential back-impacts, rather than being drawn from numeric scales as was the case for your assessments of Probability and Impact.

What Data is Added to the Risk Log During Risk Severity Assessment?

The following areas should be addressed and entered into your Risk Log before you move from Severity Assessment into later stages of Risk Management:

- **Probability**. Enter the probability value (High, Medium or Low) that you determined for the Risk using the Risk Probability Table (see the example at Figure 3.).

- **Impact**. Record the impact assessment (High, Medium or Low) you determined for the Risk using the Impact Assessment Key (see the example at Figure 4.).

- **Risk Severity Level**. Enter the value for Risk Severity Level (Level 1, Red; Level 2, Yellow or Level 3, Blue) that you derived from the Risk Severity Grid (see the example at Figure 5.).

- **Pre-Occurrence Manifestation**. Enter narrative statements regarding the potential for effects on team morale, behavior or performance arising from awareness of the existence of the Risk.

Risk Severity Assessment - Roundup

On your first pass through the Rapid Rollout Methodology for Project Risk Management, once you have carried out Step 2, Risk Severity Assessment, you will have a number of Risks in your Risk Log with by now a fair amount of data for each Risk. Risks will have Titles, Descriptions, and Serial Numbers, and Risks will be assigned to Categories. Additionally each Risk will have ratings for Probability and Impact, as well as an overall Severity Level assessment. You may also have captured information regarding any Pre-Occurrence Manifestation of the Risks.

Even before moving into Risk Response Formulation, Step 3 in the Methodology, you can sort, group and analyze the "universe" of Risks within your Risk Log. You can use the Risk Log as a communication tool to explain to stakeholders just what the overall level of threat, and opportunity, is within and around your project. This can help senior management make strategic decisions with regard to your project. It can also help you make a case for increased funding or for higher priority to be given to your project within the organization.

Of course, you do have to start thinking about what to DO about your Risks as well, so let's move to the next step in the Methodology, Step 3, Risk Response Formulation.

Chapter Postscript: Quantitative Risk Modeling

As discussed in this Chapter, Sir Ganttalot's Rapid Rollout Methodology condenses the key elements of Qualitative Risk Analysis and Quantitative Risk Analysis into a single Methodology Step: Step 2 –Risk Severity Assessment. This decision reflects many years of experience in actually rolling out Risk Management Approaches in different types of projects and organizations. When aiming to deploy a methodology rapidly, delving into too much detail in every area of the field of Risk Management can mean that you get bogged down and never really make true headway.

Nevertheless, there is much value to be gained from expanding into some form of Quantitative Analysis of your Risks, possibly by performing statistical modeling of Risk Impact across your project through the use of Monte Carlo simulation. Sir Ganttalot® encourages those readers with interest in this specific aspect of Risk Analysis to research the topic in more detail.

Chapter 5

Risk Response Formulation

Moving into this step in the Methodology you will have a Risk Log containing Risks that have been described and analyzed in some detail. You know what the Risk events are and how they will impact your project if they happen. You have assessed their probability of occurrence and the magnitude of their impact, and you have determined an overall level of severity for each Risk and determined the potential for Pre-Occurrence Manifestation. Now, you can prioritize your responses to each Risk.

Prioritizing Responses is necessary for two reasons. Firstly, some Risks are, flat out, so important that an early and vigorous Response is essential. Secondly, sad to say, we never have enough time, money or resources to do all the Risk Management we would like, so we have to allocate our efforts and resources where the effect is likely to be the greatest.

The AIM of Risk Responses

Risk Responses are intended to do something about the Risks. You are done with cataloging and analyzing; now you need to plan your reaction to each Risk.

Before proceeding further with this discussion I must once again remind you that Risks can be Positive as well as Negative. The consequences of uncertain events could be beneficial or harmful; they could represent Threats or Opportunities. Risk Responses should focus on containing Threats, and pursuing Opportunities.

Primary Responses, Contingency Responses and Fallback Responses

For the most severe Risks in our Risk Register, the Level 1 (Red) Risks, Sir Ganttalot's recommended methodology calls for you to develop Primary Responses, Contingency Responses, and Fallback Responses.

For your Level 2 (Yellow) Risks you might develop Primary Responses and Contingency Responses only.

CHAPTER 5: RISK RESPONSE FORMULATION

For your Level 3 (Blue) Risks, you may simply move these to a "Watch List" area of your Risk Log, and take no further action unless Risk Review (Step 5 of the Methodology) indicates that the severity has increased.

So what do we mean by each of these response types? Here's the answer:

- **Primary Responses** are the actions that you plan and then carry out to directly *address* a Risk. You are formulating approaches to contain the Threats posed by Negative Risks and to pursue the Opportunities presented by Positive Risks.

- **Contingency Responses** are activities you plan in advance that you will carry out if the Risk actually happens. These are the actions necessary to deal with the *consequences* of the occurrence of the Risk. In other words you plan ahead what you will do if the Risk becomes a real live project Issue.

- **Fallback Responses** are again activities planned ahead of time, but you can think of them as "Plan B" responses. Fallback Responses are responses you will implement if a Risk has a higher than expected impact, or if you determine that your primary Risk Responses are not having as great an effect on the Risk as you had intended.

Types of Primary Risk Response

By far the most common term used within Project Management circles for responding to Risks is the word, "mitigation". But mitigation is only one of the possible approaches available to us. And mitigation is only an approach for Negative Risks; it is meaningless for Positive Risks.

Here is a summary of the main types of Primary Risk Responses available. We will define them first, and then illustrate them with some everyday life examples.

Possible Primary Responses for NEGATIVE (Threat) Risks

- **Mitigate** – Take action to reduce the Probability and/or reduce the potential Negative Impact of a Threat. This is by far the most common response to Negative Risks.

- **Transfer** (Deflect) – Make the Threat Risk the responsibility of a third party (make it someone else's Risk!).

- **Avoid** – Eliminate the Threat altogether.

- **Precipitate** – Make the Threat Risk actually happen. Typically you force the Risk to occur at a time of your choosing so that you can deal with it at your own convenience when you have the resources to best do so.

- **Accept** – Don't formulate any Primary Response at all. Note that there are 2 levels of "Acceptance"
    - Active Acceptance – Formulate NO Primary Response, but develop a Contingency Response that can be implemented if the Negative Risk actually happens.
    - Passive Acceptance – Take no action other than remember to review the Threat Risk for changes in the nature of the Risk or in its Severity Level.

Possible Primary Responses for POSITIVE (Opportunity) Risks

- **Enhance** – Take action to increase the Probability that the Opportunity will happen or to increase the potential benefits of the Opportunity. This is by far the most common response to Positive Risks.

- **Share** – Extend parts of the Opportunity or its benefits with a third party or partner.

- **Exploit** – Take action to ensure or guarantee that the Positive event actually takes place.

- **Precipitate** - Make the Opportunity Risk actually happen *now*, or at a time of your choosing so that you can maximize your ability to benefit from the Opportunity. This is subtly different from Exploit in that you engineer the timing of the occurrence, not simply ensure that it happens sometime.

- **Accept** – Don't formulate any Primary Response at all. Again here for Positive Risks there are 2 levels of "Acceptance"
    - Active Acceptance – Formulate NO Primary Response, but develop a Contingency Response that can be implemented if the Opportunity Risk actually happens.
    - Passive Acceptance – Take no action other than remember to review the Opportunity Risk for changes in the nature of the Risk or in its Severity Level.

CHAPTER 5: RISK RESPONSE FORMULATION

You should be able to see from these descriptions that there are 4 "matched pairs" of response types. For each type of response to a Negative Risk there is a flip-side response type for Positive Risks. These pairings are:

> **Mitigate** for Negative Risks equates to **Enhance** for Positive Risks
>
> **Transfer** for Negative Risks equates to **Share** for Positive Risks
>
> **Avoid** for Negative Risks equates to **Exploit** for Positive Risks
>
> **Precipitate** applies to **both** Negative and Positive Risks
>
> **Accept** applies to **both** Negative and Positive Risks

(**Note.** **Precipitate** is a Risk Response that seldom features in other Risk approaches. Sir Ganttalot has specifically formulated and included this particular response as one of the distinguishing characteristics of the Rapid Rollout Methodology for Project Risk Management. This is because in practice, precipitating selected Risks has proven to be a proactive approach that reduces uncertainty. Reducing uncertainty is what Risk Management is all about!)

Examples of Primary Risk Responses in Practice – Threat Risk

In order to help solidify these various "types" or Primary Risk Response, let's use a couple of practical examples of Risks, one Threat Risk and one Opportunity Risk.

For our **Threat Risk** example, here is a Risk that is similar to one you might have in your own Risk Log:

"Janet Alexander resigns from the company resulting in 6 weeks of delay in completion of testing due to the need to secure a replacement Tester and bring that person up to speed."

Types of Risk Response to the foregoing Risk might include:

- **Mitigate**. Work to reduce the *Probability* of Janet resigning by offering a retention bonus, giving her a small promotion, giving her a better office, increasing her work satisfaction, or other actions of similar kind.

    You might also work to lessen the potential *Impact* if Janet does resign anyway. You could start training up an understudy, or take other action whereby Janet's skills and knowledge get transferred at least partially to an as-needed replacement. Now, there is of course the possibility that if you simply tell Janet to "start training up John to do your job!" that the *Probability* of Janet resigning could go UP a little! She might think that something's afoot, and that sending out some resumes might be a good idea. So exercise your communication and interpersonal skills when taking such an approach! Other examples of working on reducing the potential impact (i.e. shortening the delay caused by Janet resigning) could include getting Janet's role and responsibilities, and her ongoing work results, thoroughly documented. You could also get in touch with a staffing agency and perhaps pay a small retainer such that they always have a few resumes of candidates available and pre-screened as potential replacements for Janet in the event that you need someone quickly.

- **Transfer**. For an existing staff member like Janet, the only form of Transference that might be an option for the Risk of her leaving could be some form of expensive business insurance to cover the cost of the Impact. For similar Risks regarding new staffing appointments, you could consider subcontracting the duties of that person entirely. Instead of recruiting a tester, award a testing contract. Then, word into the contract the fact that the vendor is responsible for meeting target dates, or they will incur a penalty. In fact, one of the primary purposes of contracts in a business context IS to transfer Risk.

- **Avoid**. Avoiding the Risk means to eliminate it altogether. In this example, the only feasible Avoidance strategy might be to dispense with testing altogether. Then, Janet resigning would have no impact at all. Now of course, taking this approach might eliminate one Risk, but many other Risks would now arise as a result of your decision (to do no testing). Such new Risks created as a result of controlling other Risks are referred to as "Secondary Risks", and we will discuss these at more length later in this Chapter.

- **Precipitate**. Technically, firing Janet now would be an example of Precipitation for this Risk, but it is unlikely you would take such an approach. In fact not all of the different Risk Response types will be relevant to every Risk in your Risk Log. Nevertheless in this case you could feasibly decide to remove Janet from the testing role on your project, and identify and train up one or more replacements at a time that works for you.

- **Accept**. Active Acceptance of the Risk of Janet leaving would be to do nothing at all as a Primary Response, but to put in place a

Contingency Response. (See later in this Chapter for discussion relating to planning and budgeting for Contingency Responses). Passive acceptance would simply be to do nothing at all other than monitor the Risk (and perhaps monitor Janet's level of contentment with her job).

Examples of Primary Risk Responses in Practice – Opportunity Risk

For our **Opportunity Risk** example we will use the following Risk scenario, which relates to a project to roll out a new Project Management software application within a *single* division of a company:

"Other company divisions request rollout of our Project Management software, leading to increased benefits and efficiencies company-wide."

Types of Risk Response to the foregoing Opportunity Risk might include:

- **Enhance**. Work to increase the *Probability* of other divisions wanting your software, perhaps by holding "Lunch and Learn" sessions, visiting Division Heads to explain your initiative, or by writing articles about your software in the Company Newsletter.

    You might also work to increase the potential *Benefits* of wider rollout if other Divisions deploy the software. You could maybe allow some potential users of the software within other departments to take up some of your training slots, or spare seats in training sessions that you have arranged for your own users.

- **Share**. In a sense this actual Opportunity Risk itself is a form of sharing. More directly a share *response* for this Risk would be to work with another development team in your own Division that is rolling out, say, a financial software application to your Division only. You could collaborate with that team, while you seek wider rollout of your PM application, to also deploy the financial application to additional Divisions.

- **Exploit**. Exploiting this Opportunity would mean ensuring you're your application is deployed more widely. To do so you could potentially "go to the top" and convince the CEO that he or she should mandate deployment of the software to additional Divisions.

- **Precipitate**. To precipitate this Opportunity (at a time of your choosing) perhaps an approach would be to simply deploy the application company-wide when you deploy it to your own team. In many organizations, deploying a software package requires the IT department to "push" a software update to each user machine. So, rather than have it pushed to your Division only you could ask for it to be pushed across the company. Then, as people find the application and want to use it, you can train them or mentor them as needed.

- **Accept**. Active Acceptance of the Opportunity of wider deployment would be to do nothing at all as a Primary Response, but to put in place a Contingency Response. (See later in this Chapter for discussion relating to planning and budgeting for Contingency Responses). Passive acceptance would simply be to do nothing at all other than monitor the Risk (and perhaps monitor other Divisions' frustration with their own Project Management Software).

We have discussed Primary Risk Responses at some length, so let's move on to consider Contingency Responses and Fallback Responses.

Contingency Risk Responses

A Contingency Response to a Risk is something you plan ahead of time regarding what you will do if a Risk (Threat or Opportunity) actually happens. For your Level 1 (Red) and Level 2 (Yellow) Risks you will always develop Contingency Responses in addition to your Primary Responses.

Perhaps the most important thing to bear in mind is that there is NO point formulating a Contingency Response unless, when you need to implement that response, you will have the time, money and resources you need to perform the actions associated with your response. So how on earth can you ensure that you have made allowance for actions that may never be necessary in the first place? Risks are *uncertain*, are they not? And exactly how much time, money and resources should you allocate for those uncertainties that DO come to pass and for which you WILL need funds, time and resources? What a conundrum!

The answer to all of these challenges is to ensure that during your Project Estimating and Budgeting activities that you identify and allocate **Contingency Reserves.** A common every day English definition for Contingency Reserves is, "*time, money and resources set aside to deal with known unknowns*". Now, "*known unknowns*" basically means Risks that you have identified. So in Risk Management terms, the term Contingency

Reserves simply means the funding, time and resources you will use to implement your Contingency Responses when and if you need to do so.

You also need to know that, typically, Contingency Reserves for time and money are considered part of the project Cost and Schedule baselines. And again, typically, a Project Manager can draw down, or spend, from the Contingency Reserve budgets without needing to seek approval to do so. In other words, the PM plans and allocates Contingency Reserves, and uses them, at his or her discretion.

So much for the concept. But how do you know how much money and time, or how many resources, to set aside? The approach most commonly used, and a very effective approach it is, is **called Expected Monetary Value (EMV) Analysis**. And the good news is that your Risk Log already contains much of the information you need to perform effective EMV Analysis.

Conducting Expected Monetary Value (EMV) Analysis

The base formula for EMV Analysis for a particular Risk is:

> EMV = [Risk Probability] X [VALUE of the Risk Impact]
>
> In the above formula we can separately address impacts on Cost, Time and Resources as appropriate.

To illustrate the EMV concept let's consider again that Threat Risk regarding Janet resigning, *"Janet Alexander resigns from the company resulting in 6 weeks of delay in completion of testing due to the need to secure a replacement Tester and bring that person up to speed."*

We have not discussed a Contingency Response for this Risk yet, but such a response might be, if Janet actually does resign, then at that point to pay for training for an alternate team member to equip him or her to do the testing in place of Janet. This will take time (6 weeks per you Risk Log entry) and it will cost money. To perform EMV analysis you need to analyze the Risk just a little more than you have done so far. You need a Cost Impact. Let's say you estimate the training will cost $15,000.00 in total. So now you have "values" for two types of impact, impact on time of 6 weeks and an impact on cost of $15,000.00. Now you have <u>half</u> of what you need to plug into formulas to determine EMV for Cost and EMV for Time:

> Cost EMV = [Risk Probability] X [$15,000.00]
>
> Time EMV = [Risk Probability] X [6 Weeks]

But those formulas are only half complete. You need a specific value for Risk Probability, so again you need to dig slightly deeper into the Risk. In your Risk Log, you allocated a Probability of Medium for this Risk. The Risk Probability Table at Figure 3, Chapter 4 indicates that Medium Probability equates to a Probability of between 33% and 67%. In your formulas though, you really need a single number for Probability, not a range. So at this point you have a choice of approaches:

- Adopt a policy whereby for EMV Analysis you assign a specific standard percentage probability for each of the three levels, possibly 15% for Low Probability Risks; 50% for Medium Probability Risks and 80% for High Probability Risks, or

- Revisit each Risk and determine a specific, refined, Probability % Value. This second approach is Sir Ganttalot's recommendation.

For the example Risk, let's assume you revisit and refine the Probability from Medium to a specific number, say 40%. Now, your EMV formulas for Cost EMV and Time EMV are complete:

Cost EMV = 40% X $15,000.00 = $6,000.00

Time EMV = 40% X 6 Weeks = 2.4 Weeks

For this Risk then, you would allocate into Contingency Reserve a Dollar sum of $6,000.00 and a Time amount of 2.4 Weeks.

But hold on a moment! If the Risk happens and Janet leaves, you need $15,000 to train someone, not $6,000.00. And it will take 6 weeks to train the replacement, not 2.4 weeks. So you don't have enough money or time allocated! And if Janet does NOT resign, you don't need anything at all. So you have excess funds of $6,000.00 and excess time reserve of 2.4 weeks sitting in your Contingency Reserve buckets that will not be needed at all! So what's going on here? How can I be telling you to use EMV Analysis to calculate Contingency Reserves, when even with a simple example of just one Risk I have proved to you that the concept is flawed?

The answer is also a question. How many projects do you know that have just ONE Risk? None! On a project with dozens of Risks, some will happen, and some won't happen. If you perform EMV Analysis consistently and comprehensively, you will almost certainly have very close to the right amounts of time and money in your Contingency Reserves. Furthermore, for POSITIVE Risks, your Opportunities, you can take money and time back

OUT of your Contingency Reserves in the amount of the appropriate EMV for the POSITIVE Impacts.

Fallback Risk Responses

A Fallback Response to a Risk can be thought of as a "Plan B". Such responses are planned ahead of time as backup plans in the event that your Primary Responses do not have the anticipated effect on the Risk. They are also backups to Contingency Responses in the sense that you will implement them if the Impact of a Risk turns out to be higher than anticipated. For your Level 1 (Red) Risks you will always develop Fallback Responses in addition to your Primary Responses and Contingency Responses.

Having Fallback Responses planned in advance is excellent, but you will need to know when and if they turn out to be necessary. The 4th and 5th steps in the Rapid Rollout Methodology – Step 4, Risk Control and Step 5, Risk Review will both help you determine whether you should be implementing Fallback Responses for any of your Risks. This will become apparent as you read the next two Chapters of this book.

Responding to Risk Pre-Occurrence Manifestation.

Just as it requires general management skills and discernment to *Assess* any Pre-Occurrence Manifestations of a Risk (see Chapter 4), determining what to do about such back-impacts can be equally challenging. Remember, Pre-Occurrence Manifestation refers to potential effects on team morale, behavior and performance that merely being aware of a Risk might be having on your team. Therefore, to determine responses and containment approaches for such behavior you need to consider how you can change the attitude of your team. This is not easy, and your overall project and general management skills will need to come to the fore. Because your approach does need to be *your* approach on a case-by-case basis, it is not appropriate for this book to offer more detailed guidance with regard to how you should address and contain Pre-Occurrence Manifestation of your own Risks.

Selecting Primary Responses, Contingency Responses and Fallback Responses for YOUR Risks

We have now looked at various types of possible responses to Risks. But *your* Risk Log has actual Risks for *your* project recorded in it. You need to determine what specific responses you will adopt for each of your Risks.

Just as no single set of Risks or any individual Risk always applies to every project, not all types of Risk Responses will be relevant or appropriate for a particular Risk. Furthermore, much as you would probably like to be able to do everything possible to address every single one of your Risks, the reality is that you simply don't have unlimited funds, time or resources to spend on Risk Management. You have other things that you need to spend time and money on! In addition to all of your Project Management tasks and activities, you also need to get on and do the work in the project itself. Most of the time on a project then, you will need to be judicious and selective when determining which Primary Responses, Fallback Responses and Contingency Responses make most sense for your project, and which will give the biggest "bang for the buck".

Selecting the correct and best responses is an art as well as a science. To do so effectively you need to understand your project and its stakeholders very thoroughly indeed. Accordingly, because the Rapid Rollout Methodology for Project Risk Management can apply to all types of project, and because all specific projects are unique with their own sets of Risks, circumstances and stakeholders, we will not suggest here what specific responses you should formulate. That is *your* job to do!

Remember of course that simply documenting a Risk Response and entering it into your Risk Log does not mean that it will magically implement itself. You must clearly assign responsibility for implementing response actions to named individuals. And you must communicate those assignments to the individuals concerned. And, as part of Risk Control and Risk Review (steps 4 and 5 in the Rapid Rollout Methodology), you will need to monitor the progress and effectiveness of your responses.

(**Sir Ganttalot Suggestion**: actively consider deploying a Microsoft® Project Server-based Enterprise Project Management software solution within your project. One of the many advantages of doing so is that you can link Risks in your SharePoint®-based Risk Log with tasks in your project Schedule. You can also set reminders for the tasks and for the Risks, and collaborate with Risk and task assignees regarding status and progress.)

Caution: Beware of Secondary Risks!

As you formulate and deploy Risk Responses, do be aware of the possibility that taking action on one Risk can lead to the creation of completely new

Risks altogether. Likewise, addressing one Risk can result in effects on other existing Risks. This "one step removed" effect of your Risk Responses is referred to as creating Secondary Risks, and you need to be on the lookout for Secondary Risks as part of your Risk Management Methodology.

For illustration, let's consider again one of the examples of a Risk we addressed earlier, *"Janet Alexander resigns from the company resulting in 6 weeks of delay in completion of testing due to the need to secure a replacement Tester and bring that person up to speed."* One of the possible mitigation responses we discussed was training an understudy so that he or she could get up to speed quickly if Janet resigns. Let's say that you take this approach and train John with some of Janet's skills. You have potentially created a brand new Risk, i.e. that John might take his newly-acquired skills and seek work at another company, leaving a vacancy in John's primary position that you now need to fill.

So what should you do about Secondary Risks? Well, quite simply you need to treat them like any other Risk and subject them to the full Rapid Rollout Methodology. Of course the best response is to create as few Secondary Risks as possible in the first place. When selecting Risk Responses for your initial Risks, chose responses that create the fewest possible number of Secondary Risks.

Risk Response Formulation - Roundup

Your Risk Log entry will now be pretty detailed for any Risks for which you have completed Risk Response Formulation. In addition to the results of Risk Identification and Risk Analysis, your Risks will have details of how you are planning to actually do something about the Risks. Primary Responses and possibly Contingency Responses and Fallback Responses depending on the Risk Severity Level, will be listed in the Risk Log. Your Primary Responses will be assigned to responsible parties for implementation. Any specific responses to instances of Pre-Occurrence Manifestation of Risks may also appear in your Risk Log.

In addition you will have allocated Contingency Reserve budgets for time and cost to give you the ability to implement your Contingency Responses in the event that any of the Risks actually happen. (**Note**. You may choose to add columns to the Risk Log to detail the exact amount of Contingency Reserves allocated for each Risk, or you may choose to track Contingency Reserves in a separate document altogether. There are pros and cons of both approaches. Making Reserves visible to stakeholders might give them a

PROJECT RISK MANAGEMENT – A RAPID ROLLOUT METHODOLOGY

sense that they can "afford" for the Risks to happen, and take the edge off their control measures, but on the other hand you might favor an approach of "full disclosure" / openness.)

Armed with all of this analysis and planning of Risks and your responses, you now need to control the implementation of your responses and monitor the expenditure of your Contingency Reserves.

Chapter 6
Risk Control

At this stage in the Rapid Rollout Methodology for Project Risk Management you move from planning-related activities (identifying, assessing severity, and formulating responses) into a phase where you begin implementing the decisions you have made about your Risks. In particular you need to actually implement your planned Risk Responses. Like any other planned activities, however, your planned Risk Responses may not unfold as you had hoped or intended.

If you consider your Risk Log for a specific Risk at this stage in the Methodology, your Log will contain as a minimum a Description of the Risk, assessments of its Probability, Impact and overall Severity, and one or more Primary Responses, Contingency Responses and Fallback Responses. For all or those responses you will most likely also have assigned one or more individuals to take ownership of the responses and to be responsible for going ahead and implementing those responses. But here's the thing: just because you assigned Responsibility to implement some specific tasks doesn't mean that the tasks will necessarily be carried out. This applies to Risk Responses just as it does to any other task or activity on the project. You need to supervise the implementation of the responses, you need to support your staff and other stakeholders as they implement those responses, and you need to make sure that the responses are effective.

Even if cases where your planned Risk Responses are indeed being carried out, it may transpire that they do not have the intended effect on the Risks concerned. Perhaps they are having less effect than hoped. Even worse, maybe they are having detrimental effects. They could be exacerbating rather than reducing Threat Risks. They could be reducing Opportunity Risks rather than strengthening them.

As stated in the Methodology Overview section of this book (Chapter 2), Risk Control doesn't happen in isolation. It works in tandem with the next Stage in the Methodology, Risk Review. In Risk Review you will be revaluating all aspects of the Risk on a continuous basis. This involves reviewing the effectiveness of Risk Responses as well as Reviewing Risk Identification and

Risk Severity Assessment data regarding each Risk. So it is in Risk Review that you "stay on top of" Risks and Risk Responses. In THIS section of the Methodology, Risk Control, you focus on tactically implementing the Risk Responses. You will also implement Contingency and Fallback Responses if and when these prove to be necessary (i.e. if Risk Review indicates that they are needed). Likewise, if Risk Review indicates any instances of Risk Pre-Occurrence Manifestation, then Risk Control may need to kick-in to deal with the resultant effects.

Areas of Focus in Risk Control

Because Risk Control is fundamentally a matter of getting out there and implementing Risk Responses, the activities you will be carrying out are similar to those needed for delivering your overall project. More specifically, your Risk Control activities are likely to include the following:

- Ensure that team members and stakeholders who have been assigned tasks or activities related to Risk Responses (Risk Response Owners) are aware of their assignments.
- Exercise your interpersonal and management skills to ensure that Risk Response Owners and other stakeholders understand the importance of Risk Management generally and of their own Risk Responses in particular.
- Provide resources, support and guidance to assist Risk Response Owners in implementing responses.
- Update the Risk Log with details of the progress and status of the Risk Responses (enter information into the "Primary Risk Response Progress and Comments" section of the Risk Log).
- Resolve problems arising from the implementation of responses, including any conflict between responses for different Risks.
- If triggered to do so as a result of Risk Review, modify Risk Responses as needed.
- When triggered by Risk Review, implement Fallback Plans if primary Risk Responses (even after modification per the previous bullet) are proving ineffective.
- Minimize the creation of Secondary Risks.
- For Risks that actually materialize (as identified by Risk Review) implement Contingency Responses.
- Control expenditure of Contingency Reserves.

- Deal with the results or impacts of any Pre-Occurrence Manifestation of your Risks (as identified by Risk Review).

Risk Control – Roundup

Controlling Risks involves many of the same activities and management skills required to deploy any other aspect of your project. At the core of Risk Control is the tactical implementation of your Risk Responses. This requires strong skills in the areas of managing people, managing resources and resolving issues. As well as ensuring that Risk Responses are actually carried out, Risk Control responds to any need (as indicated by Risk Review) to modify Risk Responses, deploy Fallback or Contingency Responses or to deal with any Pre-Occurrence Manifestation of your Risks.

Chapter 7

Risk Review

Risk Review is a step in the Methodology, the last step in the list in fact. But you do NOT just review Risks at the end of our project. Risk Review is an ONGOING activity. As soon as you identify a single Risk you need to start a recurring Review of everything to with that Risk.

Let's revisit our diagram showing how the steps in the Rapid Rollout Methodology relate logically to one another:

Figure 6: Relationship between Risk Review and the Other Methodology Steps

From the diagram, the role of Risk Review within the Methodology becomes clear. Risk Review is the directing and coordinating step in the Methodology that orchestrates all the other steps. Let's break this apart a little and see the specific interactions between Risk Review and the other steps.

Risk Review interacts with the other Methodology Steps as follows:

- **Interaction with Risk Identification.** On a recurring basis the descriptions and characteristics of Risks in the Risk Log must be re-examined to ensure that the descriptions are still valid in light of the current status of your project. Projects change and so do the Risks associated with them. Furthermore, some Risks stop being Risks altogether. Maybe the Threat or Opportunity associated with a Risk is no longer a factor, or maybe their time has passed. You must also remember that completely new Risks can arise during your project. In short, Risk Review ensures that the Identification data for existing Risks is still valid, and also ensures that additional Risk Identification takes place on a recurring basis.

- **Interaction with Risk Severity Assessment**. Just as the descriptions and characteristics of Risks can change over time, so can the severity of the Threat or size of the Opportunity presented by each Risk. Such changes in severity can arise from changes in your project or in the environment of your project, or they might arise (and hopefully they WILL arise) as a result of your implementation of Risk Responses. In the case of Risk Mitigation or Risk Enhancement Responses in particular, such responses were specifically formulated in the first place to directly address the Probability and/or Impact of your Risks. In many ways then, *unless* the Severity of your Risks changes as a result of Risk Management, then quite possibly your Risk Responses need to be modified!

- **Interaction with Risk Response Formulation and with Risk Control**. From the diagram showing the relationship between Methodology Steps (Figure 6) you can see that Risk Response Formulation is **tactically** directed by Risk Control which is in turn **strategically** overseen by Risk Review. As Risk Responses are actually deployed in practice, you need to exercise Risk Control to enable and support the implementation of those responses. However, as the responses are implemented, they will likely modify the nature, severity and characteristics of the Risks themselves. Risk Review is the step that determines the extent to which your Risk Responses are actually having an effect on each Risk, and determines when and if a modified approach is needed. If so, additional Risk Response Formulation is carried out to determine the revised approach. Risk Control is also potentially triggered by Risk Review as to any need to implement Contingency and/or Fallback Plans. Risk Review will also help identify any Secondary Risks you might be creating, and then submit these into the overall Rapid Rollout Methodology just as for any other Risk. Lastly, Risk Review is the mechanism whereby any additional instances of Pre-Occurrence Manifestation will be uncovered.

Additional Risk Review Activities

In addition to orchestrating the other Risk Methodology Steps, Risk Review includes some specific actions of its own. Perhaps of most significance, as part of Risk Review you will determine exactly how, when and how often the various Risks in your Risk Log will be revisited for review purposes. You might choose, for example, to hold Risk Review Workshops at specific times during the life of your project. If so, exactly what happens during each workshop will depend on your own needs, plans and decisions regarding Risk Management and overall management of your project. You may decide to include Risk Review as part of routine project Status Meetings. In such cases you will probably look at a subset of Risks during Status Meetings, maybe the Top 10 Risks, or perhaps a different set of Risks at each Status Meeting based on a program of reviews of your own devising. You could, for example, review Risks from different Categories at each meeting.

Remember also that in the event that you implement Contingency Plans for any of your Risks, then you will be tapping into your Contingency Reserves of time and money that you had set aside for this specific purpose (see "Contingency Risk Responses" in Chapter 5). The levels of Contingency Reserves must be monitored to ensure that they being consumed at the expected rate. If not, you will need to instigate action to allocate or request additional Contingency Reserves, or to reallocate or surrender any excess funds from Contingency Reserves that are now proving to be unnecessary.

Risk Reporting

Multiple stakeholders both within your project and beyond will have a natural and vested interest in the level of Risk associated with your project. Not surprisingly therefore, these people need regular information about your project Risks and about the status of your Risk Management activities.

Exactly how you go about reporting Risk information will depend on the nature and needs of your stakeholders. Some general guidelines are given below, but do treat these as guidelines only. Also, please refer to Appendix 3 for some examples of reports and diagrams that might be useful within your own Risk Reporting strategy.

Generally, different stakeholders will find the following types of Risk Reports helpful:

- **Senior Stakeholders**. These individuals will look for summarized, high-level information about the most significant Risks on your project, and especially about Risks that apply to their specific areas of interest within your project. Perhaps a simple extract from the Risk Log showing the most important ("Top 5" or "Top 10") Risks, possibly sorted or filtered by particular Categories of Risk, will suffice. Data for each Risk should include as a minimum: *Risk Serial Number; Risk Description; Risk Category; Threat/Opportunity (T/O); Probability; Impact; Risk Severity Level; Primary Risk Response Details; Primary Risk Response Progress and Comments; Response Owner; Date Raised;* and *Status.*
- **Owners of Risk Responses**. Anyone actually assigned responsibility for Risk Response actions will need full details about those Risks. Make available to these people all detail in the Risk Log for any Risks where they "own" responses.
- **"Number Crunchers"**! As the Project Manager you will quite possibly want to analyze numeric data and trends with regard to Risks, with regard to the current and anticipated status of your Contingency Reserves, and with regard to the "modeled" individual and cumulative impact of Risks on project timescales and finances. And there will be others in your organization wanting similar, detailed, numeric data. Examples of such individuals and groups include Financial Analysts, corporate-level Risk Teams over and above your own project, organizational Project and Program Management Offices and many others. You may need a sophisticated Risk Modeling capability in order to address these. Remember, though, that this is a Rapid Rollout Methodology. Quantitative Risk Analysis represents a more in-depth component of a methodology that you can deploy as and when your overall level of Risk Management Maturity warrants it.
- **Other Stakeholders**. Your Risk Log is the repository where all information about all your Risks is maintained. You will find it very easy to extract data at a level of detail that your different stakeholders will find appropriate for their needs.

(**Sir Ganttalot Suggestion**: actively consider deploying a Microsoft® Project Server-based Enterprise Project Management software solution within your project. One of the many advantages of doing so is that you can create your project Risk Log in SharePoint®, and then link your Risks with tasks in your project Schedule. You will then have a rich reporting and tracking application whereby you set reminders for the tasks and for the Risks, collaborate with Risk and task assignees regarding status and progress, and create pre-filtered reports and views that will meet the needs of different stakeholders.

Risk Review - Roundup

Risk Review is the coordinating step in the Methodology that determines when and how the other steps will be carried out and revisited.

During Risk Review, you stay on top of all data to do with a Risk. Risk Review revisits Risk Information and updates it to reflect changes arising from the nature of the Risks and within your project and beyond. Risk Review also determines how your own Risk Management activities are impacting on Risks, particularly with regard to the impact of your Risk Responses.

Within Risk Review you also monitor your Contingency Reserves for Time and Money to determine if adjustments are needed. You also determine and implement a set of Risk Reporting Protocols to meet your stakeholders' needs for Risk information.

Chapter 8

Thoughts and Considerations for Project Risk Management

In the preceding sections of this book I have laid out the steps involved in the Rapid Rollout Methodology for Project Risk Management. Do remember that the intention has been to empower you to deploy a Risk Management approach quickly that can bring about early benefits. But Project Risk Management is a huge field. Many people are engaged solely in Project Risk Management as a specialized profession. So however much Risk Management you are carrying out, there is always a possibility to do more.

So how far do you go with all this Risk stuff? Well, as with any discipline within Project Management, it comes down to an honest assessment of the costs and benefits of taking that next step towards even more detailed Risk Management. Don't ever do "more" Risk Management as an end in itself. You must assess the true costs and benefits of doing so first. And remember that the costs and benefits themselves will depend very much on the current level of maturity in Project Management and Risk Management that is at play within and around your Project.

Take your mind back to the scenario outlined back in Chapter 1 ("Why Should You Deploy a Risk Management Methodology?"). Remember how we contrasted the obvious benefits of Risk Management with a more technical concept such as Earned Value? Well, therein is a warning to you. Don't complicate Risk Management to the point that people don't understand it or see any value in it. By all means build on the foundation laid by this Rapid Rollout Methodology, but please do so with sensitivity and in a gradual, incremental fashion.

Epilogue

Thank you for reading through this book and for considering the need for a Rapid Rollout Methodology for Risk Management within your own project. We wish you every success in your Project Management and Risk Management endeavors.

This volume is the first of a number of additional volumes covering Rapid Rollout approaches for sub-disciplines within the profession of Project Management. Please keep an eye open for these additional methodologies. One way you can do this would be to subscribe to Sir Ganttalot® on YouTube®, where we will announce new books and methodology products as they become available.

You are also very welcome to email the author at info@westallmurray.com.

Appendix 1

A Possible Schedule for Rolling Out Risk Management

The Chapters in this book explain in detail the steps in the Rapid Rollout Methodology for Project Risk Management. In doing so, however, we have described the Methodology in terms of an environment where the Methodology is deployed and in operation. So, how do you go from a situation of no Risk Management at all, to one where the Methodology is up and running? Well, as always it depends on many factors specific to your organization and its overall level of Project Management maturity, but you may find the following set of actions helpful as an initial roadmap for your own deployment.

Day 1

- Create your Risk Log in Excel, SharePoint, or similar software application or database.

Days 2-3

- Enter your own starter set of 10 Risks. Take those 10 Risks through the steps of Risk Identification, Risk Severity Assessment and Risk Response Formulation, and update your Risk Log with associated data at each stage.
- Select 5-10 target stakeholders to review your starter Risks and whom you would like to participate in your first Risk Workshop.
- Create an agenda for a Risk Workshop. Include as agenda items for the session a review of the starter set of Risks as well as a Brainstorming session for identification of additional Risks.
- Distribute meeting invitations and the Agenda for the first Risk Workshop.
- Allow 5 days for invitees to get ready for the workshop. Some will have questions for you, so be prepared to meet with one or more stakeholders to gear them up for the workshop.

Day 8

- Hold the first Risk Workshop. Explain Risk Management and your vision for its deployment on your project. Follow the agenda to review the starter set of Risks and to capture additional Risks.

Day 9

- Pull together the mass of information from the Risk Workshop. Screen, consolidate and reconcile captured information to create a "Version 2" Risk Log with your expanded set of Risks.
- Perform the steps of Risk Severity Assessment and Risk Response Formulation on the Risks.

Day 10

- Implement Risk Control on your Risks. Specifically, ensure that all Risk Response actions are communicated to the people responsible for implementing them. Expect some push-back! Respond with your full arsenal of management and interpersonal skills, but take advice where needed if the Risk Responses really DO need to be modified or reassigned.
- Circulate your Risk Register to selected senior stakeholders who were NOT involved in your Risk Workshop (the Delphi approach) seeking input/comment/guidance. Allow 3 days for feedback.

Days 11-13

- Formulate your Risk Review strategy. Determine timings of ongoing Risk activities to include:
    - Your own review of Risks and Risk Responses.
    - Risk Reviews by other stakeholders (perhaps hold scheduled Risk Workshops, or include Risks as a topic at each project status meeting).
- Determine formats and frequency for Risk Reports for various stakeholders.

Day 14

- Incorporate any modifications or updates resulting from Delphi feedback (see Day 10, second item).
- Implement your Risk Review strategy, including an ongoing revisiting of all the other methodology steps (Risk Identification, Risk Severity Assessment, Risk Response Formulation, and Risk Control.

End of Month 3

- Perform a comprehensive review of how well the Methodology is meeting your needs for Risk Management within your project. Apply modifications as needed.

Month 4 through to the End of your Project

- Continue Risk Management activities.
- Reap the benefits of your hard work!

Appendix 2

Example of a Risk Log

This example illustrates a "Single Form per Risk" style of Risk Log. Such a format is likely to be used within a Risk log built on a database or collaboration-type application (SharePoint® for example). Summarized views of all or selected Risks can be created separately within such applications. If your preference is to use a spreadsheet application, then each of the "fields" of data in this example would appear as spreadsheet columns.

Risk Serial Number	073
Risk Title	Janet Resigns
Risk Description	*Janet Alexander resigns from the company resulting in 6 weeks of delay in completion of testing due to the need to secure a replacement Tester and bring that person up to speed.*
Risk Category	Human Resources
Threat/Opportunity (T/O)	T
Probability	Medium
Impact	High
Pre-Occurrence Manifestation	We are not fully challenging Janet and not getting full value of her skills because of reluctance to "tick her off" and trigger a resignation.
Risk Severity Level	Level 2 / Yellow
Trigger (optional)	Janet submits her notice (2 weeks, as per hiring agreement)
Primary Risk Response Type	Mitigate

APPENDIX 2: EXAMPLE OF A RISK LOG

Primary Risk Response Details	1. Reduce *Probability* by offering Janet a $10K retention bonus contingent upon staying on the project through deployment. 2. Reduce *Impact* by "retaining" ACME Universal Staffing Solutions to always have 5+ resumes of potentially qualified candidates available.
Primary Risk Response Progress and Comments	1. Spoke with HR and Accounts to ensure that the retention bonus is permitted. 2. In discussion with ACME regarding retainer fee (current quote of $2K appears excessive).
Response Owner	1. Peter Perfect. 2. Helen Troy.
Contingency Response	Bring over the best-qualified available Tester "on loan" from any other project in the overall program.
Fallback Response	TBD, but may include an increased retention bonus.
Date Raised	Jan 27, 2014.
Status	Open.
Date Closed	-

Appendix 3

Examples of Charts, Diagrams, and Reports used in Risk Management

You may find some of the following artifacts helpful in support of various stages of the Rapid Rollout Methodology for Project Risk Management.

Cause and Effect / Ishikawa / Mind-Map – Style Diagrams

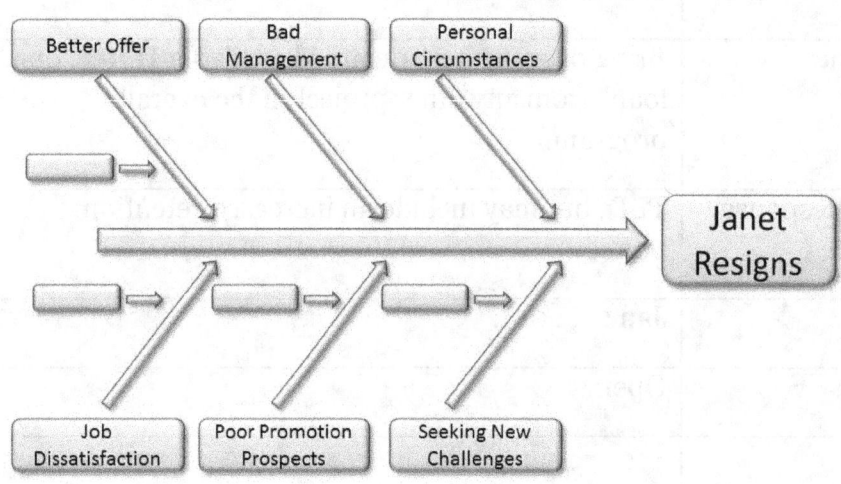

Diagrams of this type can help you back-track from a headline Risk event to look for underlying or contributory causes for the Risk. They may prove useful during Risk Identification.

Multiple variations on this theme exist. The type illustrated is an Ishikawa or Cause and Effect diagram. Sometimes this may be referred to as a Fishbone diagram because of its appearance. A similar diagram, where the main event or circumstance is placed centrally, with radiating causes and sub-causes, would be more akin to a Mind Map diagram.

APPENDIX 3: EXAMPLES OF RISK MANAGEMENT CHARTS, DIAGRAMS, AND REPORTS

A Risk Breakdown Structure (RBS)

A Risk Breakdown Structure (RBS) is likely to be an "evolving" artifact. It depicts the relationship between, and a hierarchy of, the Risk Categories you have selected for your Risk Log. You might start off with a simple RBS to help jump-start the identification of specific Risks for your project. Then, as you move into Risk Identification and other steps in the Methodology, additional Categories may prove to be needed. You may also change the RBS if you find that some Categories don't apply to your project, or you might decide to consolidate or even split out or expand Categories.

Remember as well that this diagram and other artifacts you produce might prove very useful to you and to other project managers on future projects. So save your RBS, your Risk Log and any Risk Reports for posterity as part of what the Project Management Institute® refers to as "Organizational Process Assets".

Tornado Diagrams

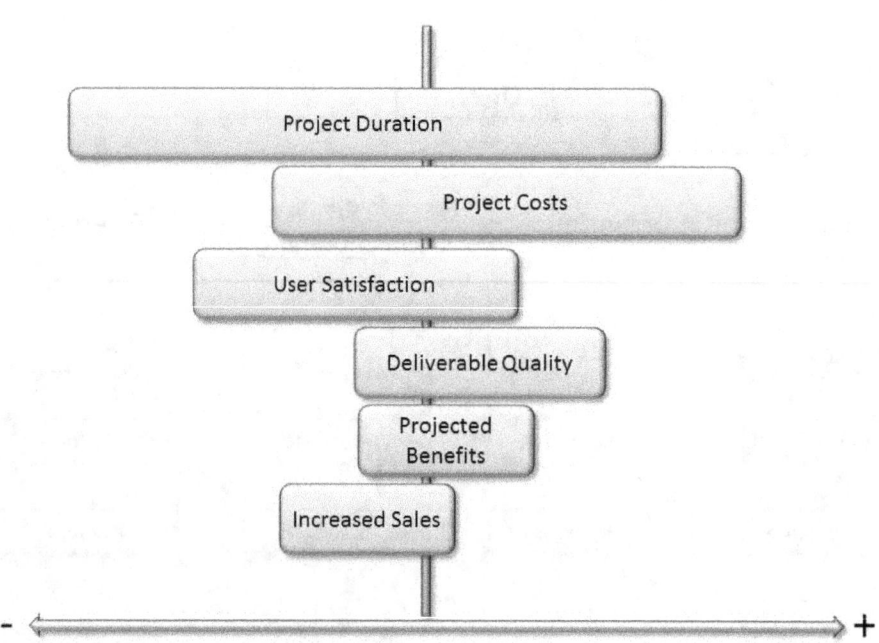

These diagrams have multiple uses. Within Risk Management they are most frequently used as part of Risk Severity Assessment to illustrate the extent to which a particular Risk might have Positive or Negative impacts on specific project or task "variables", such as Time, Cost, Scope, Quality, etc. This type of analysis is known as "Sensitivity Analysis".

In your own project you will probably use some form of percentage scale for the bottom axis on the diagram, as the variables will all have different numeric units such as Dollars, Weeks, Error Rates and more. Place the variables in descending order on the vertical axis in terms of total range of impact, and end up with a rough resemblance to a tornado!

"Top 5" or "Top 10" and Similar Risk Reports

There will be many occasions (Risk Workshops, Project Status Meetings) where you will want to present and/or discuss the current status of the most significant Risks in your Risk Log. Typically on such occasions you won't have time to discuss all your Risks, and even for your Top 5 or Top 10 you won't have time to address every entry in every cell of your Risk Log. For

APPENDIX 3: EXAMPLES OF RISK MANAGEMENT CHARTS, DIAGRAMS, AND REPORTS

such situations it is helpful to be able to produce an extract of selected columns from your Risk Log.

Risk Log extracts can take the form of a filtered set of columns from a Spreadsheet-style Log. If your Risk Log is instead held in SharePoint® then your Top 5 or Top 10 lists can be created as Views with filtered and grouped Risks and Columns of data.

The cells or data items you choose to display in your extract will vary depending on your review needs, and possibly based on which stakeholders are involved. You might, for example, be more restrictive in what data you show to a client than would be the case for an internal Project Status Meeting. The following set of cells/fields from the Risk Log may represent a good starter set for your own thinking regarding the data to extract for your own purposes:

- Risk Serial Number
- Risk Description
- Risk Category
- Threat/Opportunity (T/O)
- Probability
- Impact
- Risk Severity Level
- Primary Risk Response Type (Optional)
- Primary Risk Response Details
- Primary Risk Response Progress and Comments
- Response Owner
- Date Raised
- Status

Glossary / Index of Main Entries

Accept. A possible **Primary Risk Response** for both **Threat Risks** and for **Opportunity Risks** where no immediate action is planned at all. There are 2 levels of "Acceptance":

> **Active Acceptance** – Formulate NO Primary Response, but develop a **Contingency Response** that can be implemented if the Risk actually happens..42, 44, 46

> **Passive Acceptance** – Take no action other than remember to **Review** the Risk for changes in the nature of the Risk or in its **Severity Level**...42, 45, 46

Affinity Diagramming. A technique to help organize and categorize large amounts of conceptual data, such as that gathered during a **Brainstorming** session. 25

Avoid. A possible **Primary Risk Response** for **Threat Risks** where the aim is to eliminate the Threat altogether..41, 44

Brainstorming. A data gathering technique characterized by fast, no holds barred, "any idea counts" and other free-form input from multiple **Stakeholders** in a conference room or meeting location. 25

Category (Risk Category). A grouping or major area of Risk or source of Risk within your project, e.g. technology, human resources, etc. Each Risk in your **Risk Log** will be assigned to a Category. 26

Cause and Effect Diagram. Also known as a Fishbone or Ishikawa Diagram. A useful artifact to help with Identification of Risks and their contributory causes..68

Contingency Response. One or more actions planned ahead of time that you will carry out if an identified Risk actually occurs. 46

Control. (Risk Control). The step in the **Rapid Rollout Methodology** where you implement and manage your selected Risk Responses. 53

Contingency Reserves. Time and/or money set aside to deal with Risks if they actually happen. In essence, Contingency Reserves represent the time

GLOSSARY / INDEX OF MAIN ENTRIES

and money needed to fund your pre-planned **Contingency Responses**. Levels for Contingency Reserves are calculated using **Expected Monetary Value (EMV)** Analysis. 46

Consequential Uncertainty. A term used by Sir Ganttalot to characterize project Risk. "*If* situation X arises, there *will be* consequences for the project". 11

Description (Risk Description). An entry in your **Risk Log** that summarizes the nature of the **Threat** or **Opportunity** presented by the Risk and the effect the Risk will have on your project if it were to occur. 26

Delphi Technique. A technique for interacting with project **Stakeholders** to capture Risk information. The technique involves one or more rounds of information collection individually from each. Information is then consolidated and the results circulated to all submitters for additional comment. 24

Enhance. A possible **Primary Risk Response** for **Opportunity Risks** where the aim is to take action to increase the **Probability** that the Opportunity will happen or to increase the potential benefits of the Opportunity. 42, 45

Expected Monetary Value (EMV). A numeric value calculated by multiplying a Risk's **Probability** by its anticipated **Impact** on project cost or schedule. EMV analysis is used to determine required levels of **Contingency Reserves**. 47

Exploit. A possible **Primary Risk Response** for **Opportunity Risks** where the aim is to take action to ensure or guarantee that the Positive event actually takes place. This is subtly different from Precipitate in that you do not engineer the timing of the occurrence, but simply ensure that it happens sometime. 42, 45

Fallback Response. One or more actions planned ahead of time that you will take if your **Primary Risk Responses** do not have sufficient effect, or if a Risk occurs and the **Impact** is greater than expected. You can think of Fallback Responses as "Plan B" responses. 49

Fishbone Diagram. Another name for a **Cause and Effect** or **Ishikawa Diagram**. 68

PROJECT RISK MANAGEMENT – A RAPID ROLLOUT METHODOLOGY

Identification (Risk Identification). The step in the **Rapid Rollout Methodology** where you capture, catalogue and record within your **Risk Log** basic information about the nature of the Risk events within your project. 21

Impact. A measure of the consequences that a Risk event will have on your project in the event that the Risk actually happens. Impact can be both Negative and Positive for particular Risks. 34

Impact Assessment Key. A table that allows you to allocate **Impact** ratings based on the likely effect of a **Risk** on major aspects of your project, primarily Cost, Schedule and Scope. 35

Ishikawa Diagram. Another name for a **Cause and Effect** or **Fishbone Diagram**. 68

Mind Map Diagram. A variation on a **Cause and Effect, Fishbone** or **Ishikawa Diagram** where the main Risk is placed centrally, with causes and sub-causes radiating outwards. 68

Mitigate. A possible **Primary Risk Response** for **Threat Risks** where the aim is to take action to reduce the **Probability** and/or reduce the potential Negative **Impact** of a Threat. 41, 43

Negative Risk. Also known as a **Threat Risk**. A **Risk** where the impact, if the Risk occurs, will be detrimental to your project...............................10

Opportunity Risk. Also known as a **Positive Risk**. A **Risk** where the impact, if the Risk occurs, will be beneficial to your project.....................10

Organizational Process Assets (OPA's). A term used to describe various documents, processes and procedures that reflect how your organization *normally* approaches projects. By implementing Risk Management, you will be improving, adding to and updating OPA's! 69

Owner (Risk or Risk Response Owner). An individual **Stakeholder** or group that has been assigned responsibility for implementing specific Risk responses for specific Risks. 54

PMBOK® Guide. "A Guide to the Project Management Body of Knowledge". A book published by the **PMI®** explaining the knowledge

GLOSSARY / INDEX OF MAIN ENTRIES

necessary to carry out effectively the most commonly encountered Project Management processes. 8

PMI® (Project Management Institute®). The world's leading professional organization for Project Management (www.pmi.org). 8

Positive Risk. Also known as an **Opportunity Risk**. A **Risk** where the impact, if the Risk occurs, will be beneficial to your project......................10

Precipitate. A possible **Primary Risk Response** for both **Threat Risks** and for **Opportunity Risks** where the aim is to force the Risk to occur at a time of your choosing so that you can deal with it or benefit from it at your own convenience when you have the resources to best do so. 42, 44, 45

Pre-Occurrence Manifestation. A concept unique to the Rapid Rollout Methodology whereby a Risk may already be having an effect on your project (on morale, team behavior or project performance) simply because **Stakeholders** are aware of the Risk's existence. 31, 37

Primary Risk Response. One or more selected approaches to directly address a Risk. For **Threat Risks**, primary response types include **Mitigate, Transfer, Avoid, Precipitate** and **Accept**. For **Opportunity Risks**, primary response types include **Enhance, Share, Exploit, Precipitate** and **Accept**..40, 41

Probability. A measure of the likelihood of a specific Risk event actually occurring. 32

Project Management Plan (PMP). A collection of documents prepared and updated as necessary throughout your project which represents the formal, approved approach to all aspects of Project Management for your project. 20

Qualitative Risk Analysis. An overall determination of the magnitude of a Risk whereby the **Probability** and **Impact** of the Risk are determined using some form of rating scale. In the **Rapid Rollout Methodology**, Qualitative Risk Analysis is combined with some limited **Quantitative Risk Analysis** within a single step called Risk **Severity Assessment**.........30

Quantitative Risk Analysis. An assessment of the specific impact that an occurrence of a Risk would have on project schedule and budget (e.g. how many weeks of delay, how many extra dollars needed). In the **Rapid**

Rollout Methodology, Quantitative Risk Analysis is combined with some limited **Qualitative Risk Analysis** within a single step called Risk **Severity Assessment**. 30

Quantitative Risk Modeling. An extended form of **Quantitative Risk Analysis** whereby the possible cumulative range of **Impacts** of one or more Risks is simulated to examine factors such as best case, worst case and most likely project duration and project budget requirements. 39

Rapid Rollout Methodology. An approach to deploying individual Project Management disciplines which focusses on bringing tangible, self-evident benefits in the quickest possible timeframe. 8

Response Formulation. (Risk Response Formulation). The step in the **Rapid Rollout Methodology** where you decide how to respond to, or deal with, the **Threat** or **Opportunity** presented by a Risk. You do this by determining **Primary Responses**, **Contingency Responses** and **Fallback Responses** as necessary and appropriate for each Risk........40

Review. (Risk Review). The step in the **Rapid Rollout Methodology** where you "stay on top of" the entire universe of **Risk Management** activities you are performing as part of the Methodology. 56

Risk. An uncertain occurrence or situation which, if it happens, will impact your project. Risk events represent the "*consequential uncertainty*" of your project..10

Risk Breakdown Structure (RBS). A diagram showing a "family tree" of **Risk Categories** within your project. It supports both **Identification** and also classification of Risks. 69

Risk Log. The master repository for identification, catalogue and status information for your project Risks and selected **Risk Responses**..........21

Risk Management. The discipline of actively addressing areas of *consequential uncertainty* within your project....................................11

Risk Management Planning. Determining the specific approach to **Risk Management** that you will adopt for your project(s). This includes assessing how much Risk Management is necessary and how you will perform it. In particular it involves the tailoring of this **Rapid Rollout Methodology** to meet your specific needs. 19

GLOSSARY / INDEX OF MAIN ENTRIES

Risk Probability Table. A table you prepare and use in support of Risk **Severity Assessment** to allocate a value for Risk **Probability**. 33

Risk Severity Grid. A table you prepare and use in support of Risk **Severity Assessment** to determine Risk **Severity Level**. 37

Secondary Risk. One or more new or additional Risks that arise entirely as a result of your responses to other Risks. 50

Sensitivity Analysis. Determining the extent to which specific aspects of your project (time, cost, etc.) would be to the occurrence of a specific Risk. Sensitivity Analysis can be facilitated through the use of **Tornado Diagrams**. 25, 70

Severity Assessment (Risk Severity Assessment). The step in the **Rapid Rollout Methodology** where you determine the extent of a **Threat** or **Opportunity** presented by a Risk. The step combines elements of **Qualitative Risk Analysis** and **Quantitative Risk Analysis**. 29

Severity Level (Risk Severity Level). A broad level of combined **Probability** and **Impact** of a Risk that allows you to assign levels of priority for your attention to each Risk. In the Rapid Rollout Methodology, three levels are used: Level 1 (Red) Risks, Level 2 (Yellow) Risks and Level 3 (Blue) Risks. 36

Share. A possible **Primary Risk Response** for **Opportunity Risks** where the aim is to take action to extend parts of the Opportunity or its benefits to a third party or partner. 42, 45

Sir Ganttalot®. A trainer, consultant and presenter on various Project Management topics, known to many from his YouTube® series of instructional videos. 7

Stakeholder. Anyone with a "vested interest" in your project, typically an individual or group who may be impacted by your project, or who has influence over your project. 23

Starter Set of Risks. An initial list of 5 to 10 Risks identified, assessed and entered into the **Risk Log** by you, used to catalyze Risk input from project **Stakeholders**. 22

Status (Risk Status). A value assigned to each Risk to indicate whether it is Open, Closed, Under Review or any of such similar designations you are using in your **Risk Log** for tracking purposes. 28

Threat Risk. Also known as a **Negative Risk**. A Risk where the impact, if the Risk occurs, will be detrimental to your project. 10

Tornado Diagram. A method of depicting the results of Sensitivity Analysis whereby the areas of the project likely to experience the largest range of Impacts are placed highest on a vertical central axis...................70

Transfer (Deflect). A possible **Primary Risk Response** for **Threat Risks** where the aim is to make the Threat Risk the responsibility of a third party. 41, 44

Trigger (Risk Trigger). An event or situation that will indicate that an identified Risk is now occurring, or is about to occur. 27

Westall Murray International, Inc. (www.westallmurray.com) Provider of Project Management solutions, consulting, training and staffing services to organizations and companies worldwide. 7

Workshops and Working Groups. Gatherings of **Stakeholders** at various points of the methodology to support specific steps (e.g. **Risk Identification, Risk Severity Assessment, Risk Review**). 18, 24

www.ingramcontent.com/pod-product-compliance
Lightning Source LLC
Chambersburg PA
CBHW080952170526
45158CB00008B/2451